THE
FLAME
OF SACRED LOVE

Text copyright © Brother Ramon SSF 1999

The author asserts the moral right
to be identified as the author of this work

Published by
The Bible Reading Fellowship
First Floor, Elsfield Hall
15–17 Elsfield Way, Oxford OX2 8FG
ISBN 1 84101 037 5

First published 1999
10 9 8 7 6 5 4 3 2

Acknowledgments
Unless otherwise stated, scripture quotations are taken from the *New
Revised Standard Version* of the Bible, copyright © 1989 by the Division
of Christian Education of the National Council of the Churches of
Christ in the USA. Used by permission.

Scriptures quoted from the Good News Bible published by The Bible
Societies/HarperCollins Publishers Ltd, UK © American Bible Society
1966, 1971, 1976, 1992, used with permission.

Extracts from the Authorized Version of the Bible (The King James
Bible), the rights in which are vested in the Crown, are vested in the
Crown, are reproduced by permission of the Crown's patentee,
Cambridge University Press.

A catalogue record for this book is available from the British Library

Printed in Singapore by Craft Print International Ltd

THE
FLAME
OF SACRED LOVE

BROTHER RAMON

The divine fire in human experience

For Michael Mitton,
channel of God's healing grace,
with gratitude

CONTENTS

The flame of sacred love

O Thou who camest from above
The pure celestial fire to impart,
Kindle a flame of sacred love
On the mean altar of my heart.

There let it for Thy glory burn
With inextinguishable blaze,
And trembling to its source return
In humble prayer and fervent praise.

Jesus, confirm my heart's desire
To work, and speak, and think for Thee;
Still let me guard the holy fire,
And still stir up Thy gift in me.

Ready for all Thy perfect will,
My acts of faith and love repeat,
Till death Thy endless mercies seal,
And make the sacrifice complete.

Charles Wesley, 1707–88

PROLOGUE

THE PURE CELESTIAL FIRE

Charles Wesley's hymns are full of fire and love! When I looked up my favourite, 'O Thou Who Camest From Above', in my treasured 1779 collection, I found that the inspiration for the hymn was found in the instructions concerning the altar of sacrifice in Leviticus 6:13: 'A perpetual fire shall be kept burning on the altar; it shall not go out.'

Terrestrial fire symbolizes celestial fire. In other words, fire is a universal symbol, one of the four elements constituting the universe, sacred in primitive cultures and common to the rituals of the world's religions—and it speaks of the divine mystery and purification.

The trail of fire runs throughout the Old and New Testaments, and our hymnology is full of its searing glory, typifying both the scorching holiness of God and the warm comfort of the indwelling Spirit. It is to be treasured, guarded and feared. Fire is dangerous and not to be played with. A human being baptized in the fire of the Holy Spirit may experience the conflagration of power in holiness, wonder and glory, but it must be accompanied by a profound godly fear. The divine fire may sear the soul, and our attitude in approaching the flame must be that of Moses before the burning bush, when the Lord said: 'Come no closer! Remove the sandals from your feet, for the place on which you are standing is holy ground' (Exodus 3:5).

The pattern of this book is based upon Wesley's hymn, with dimensions of Orthodox, Catholic and Anglican spirituality. It is not simply a book of information but of warm devotion, a sharing of those experiences in prayer to and love for God by which both the Wesley brothers were transformed—the fire of God producing a burning heart.

The first section emphasizes the altar of the heart, on which the fire is kindled. It begins with conversion, in which the soul is turned from sin to holiness, with a deepening of the life of scripture, prayer and discipline, providing the fuel by which the fire is sustained.

The second section speaks of the source of the divine fire—God himself—and the accompanying trembling which takes hold of the soul when exposed to the holy flame. Words like yearning, mystery, ecstasy, darkness and solitude are expounded in these chapters, echoing the words of Paul: '...we offer to God an acceptable worship with reverence and awe; for indeed our God is a consuming fire' (Hebrews 12:28, 29).

The third section deals with the guarding and tending of the flame. Here, we experience a heightening of the awareness of the nature of the divine fire, universal in its manifestation and yet only acknowledged and experienced by those who realize that their hearts are the altar of God. An altar empty and unattended means a life lacking in fiery glory and gentle warmth.

The final section invites the reader into the deeper reaches of prayer, where the gentle burning becomes a consuming fire, and the believer becomes united with the perfect will of God. The great saints and mystics of the Church have been illumined and set aflame with the love of God, and it has irradiated their lives and pierced the darkness of the surrounding world. In Christ, the fire of God burned most brightly, and he calls to us in those mysterious words: 'I came to bring fire to the earth, and how I wish it were already kindled!' (Luke 12:49)

The perfect will of God for his people is that they should be enveloped in the flame of his love, and enter into such a fiery union with himself that his holiness should overflow in loving compassion. Thus, men and women will be warmed, enthused and set aflame with his kindled glory.

In this section we ask what the true goal of union with God means on earth, and how we shall be carried into and beyond death, to its consummation in heaven. This is a personal and a corporate pilgrimage, for on the day of Pentecost tongues of flame appeared and rested on each one of the disciples, and they were caught up together in the enveloping fire which burned though

Jerusalem, into Samaria and the uttermost parts of the world (Acts 1:8; 2:3).

The Epilogue calls us to lay our lives on the altar of God, so that our hearts may become the altar upon which the divine fire will burn continually—to the ecstatic joy of the believer and the glory of God.

So let the fire fall!

Brother Ramon SSF
The Society of St Francis

The MEAN ALTAR of my HEART

O Thou who camest from above
The pure celestial fire to impart,
Kindle a flame of sacred love
On the mean altar of my heart.

EVANGELICAL CONVERSION

These opening chapters concern 'the mean altar of my heart', which is the place where real conversion begins. In every human being this altar exists. It is 'mean' not in the sense of narrow, spiteful and skinflint, but in the sense of simple, humble and low. Of course, the human heart may stray from the love and generosity of God, and then it does become mean in that negative sense. Because we live in a fallen world, it is common experience to find that human hearts are often closed to compassion, self-centred in orientation and narrow and exclusive in attitude. This is why conversion is essential and central in any approach to the spiritual life. We all need to be converted, and have an ongoing experience of daily conversion, not just some emotional 'high' that is divorced from the hard disciplines of daily life.

This means that conversion *may* be a 'moment' of dazzling enlightenment, when the sinner is turned from his or her selfish or evil life to the glory of the Sun of Righteousness. This was the case with Saul of Tarsus, and with many great sinners in the story of the Church. But it may also be a process of illumination along the way in which formal or dutiful religion is transformed by the light of God's grace when the human heart is touched by the Holy Spirit. Then the religion which was formerly merely a duty or a burden becomes an inexpressible joy which irradiates the whole of life, beginning a pilgrimage which is altogether new.

The place of the heart

Physiologically, the heart is the central organ of the body, the seat of physical life. When Jacob was told that Joseph his son was alive and ruling in Egypt, after years of believing that he was dead, the Hebrew text says that his heart 'fainted' (Genesis 45:26, KJV). When Eli watched the road after the great defeat of Israel's army, his heart 'trembled' (1 Samuel 4:13). The physical organ is therefore associated with psychological and spiritual symptoms, and it is often used as the centre or focus of inner, personal life. It is the spring of motivation, the seat of the passions, the centre of thought processes and the touchstone of conscience. The book of Proverbs is an abundant source of the heart as the psychological centre of emotional life as well as the seat of wisdom (Proverbs 2:10).

Jesus makes it clear that it is the pure in heart who will see God (Matthew 5:8), and that sin is first conceived and committed in the heart (Matthew 5:28). It is both the place from which evil thoughts and acts proceed, and yet the depth from which forgiveness must flow, and love for God must take root (Matthew 18:35; 22:37; Luke 18:11–15).

Thus, the appeal of the gospel is to the heart as the spring of all desires, motives and moral choices. Although the human heart is caught up in the entanglement of our fallen nature and is deceitful and sick (Jeremiah 17:9, 10), it can be cleansed, renewed and indwelt by the Holy Spirit (Psalm 51:10; Ezekiel 36:26, 27). This far-off promise in the Old Testament comes to wonderful fruition in the gospel, for it is the Holy Spirit who moves upon the stubborn human heart, cleansing, renewing and setting it ablaze with the glory of God: 'For it is the God who said, "Let light shine out of darkness", who has shone in our hearts to give the light of the knowledge of the glory of God in the face of Jesus Christ' (2 Corinthians 4:6).

Conversion as a living experience

We must not argue about whether conversion is sudden or a process experience, for it may be both. Saul was caught in a moment of crisis on the Damascus road, where he was converted once and for all (Acts 9:1–20). Yet he assured Timothy that from childhood he had known the scriptures which had made him wise to salvation (2 Timothy 3:15). There may well be a moment of enlightenment, but it is usually set within the context of a whole pattern of preparation leading up to it, and of consequences flowing from it.

The word 'synergism', meaning 'working together', is an important one here, for it means that the Holy Spirit is at work in the human heart, and that a human being responds to the divine love as he or she is moved. That is why our hearts must be open to the gracious influences of the Spirit. If you want abundant illustration outside scripture for this truth, then read the sermons of John Wesley, and sing the hymns of his brother Charles.[1]

It is intriguing to find that in the pilgrimage of John Wesley, he experienced a 'religious' conversion in 1725, and an 'evangelical' conversion in 1738. While at Christchurch, Oxford, with the wholesome teaching of his mother behind him, and the careful reading of Jeremy Taylor and Thomas à Kempis, he decided to make religion the 'business of his life'.

After ordination he returned to Oxford and, with his brother Charles, led a small band of students who were dubbed the 'Holy Club' (later 'Methodists') because of their disciplined study of scripture, their self-denial and works of charity. It was at this point that they were greatly influenced by the writings of the mystic William Law.[2]

As a dutiful religious clergyman, Wesley went as a missionary to Georgia around 1735, but the project was not a success. During a storm at sea, in which he feared for his life, he was profoundly impressed by the faith and joy of the Moravians on board, a German pietistic group who laid great emphasis on the experience of conversion and the assurance of salvation. He had conversations with the Moravian Peter Böhler, and at a Moravian meeting in Aldersgate Street, London, on 24 May 1738, studying the Letter to the Romans, he experienced his evangelical conversion, and felt his heart 'strangely warmed'. He records in his diary:

About a quarter before nine, while he was describing the change which God works in the heart through faith in Christ, I felt my heart strangely warmed. I felt I did trust in Christ, Christ alone for salvation; and an assurance was given me that he had taken away my sins, even mine, and saved me from the law of sin and death.[3]

The distinctive thing about this experience was not that he became a Christian—he had been an upright, moral and believing Christian before that, but it was a religion lacking in assurance and in what the old divines would call 'the feeling part of religion'.

What he had previously affirmed in his head now became the experience of his heart. He *felt* it to be true, and *knew* it to be real. It was a watershed experience, for there and then Christ set his heart aflame with a pure, celestial fire, and it never went out. It was not that the altar of his heart was previously heaped with rubbish or was empty, but that the poor, smouldering embers were now fanned into a flame of sacred love, and kindled so that others would catch fire from the spreading flame.

John Wesley's witness was rejected by the established Church of England, and he was reduced, at one point, to preaching from his father's gravestone. In later years he said that he never left the Church of England but that it left him, and he maintained that the world was his parish. When the first Anglican–Methodist talks were in progress some years ago, I remember Archbishop Donald Coggan saying something like: 'We rejected John Wesley once—we must not do it again.'

It is a powerful witness to Wesley's stability that after the revival which broke out among the miners of Kingswood, Bristol, in 1739, he began to organize converts into Methodist societies and bands, and led and sustained them for over fifty years. He travelled some 250,000 miles throughout Britain, preaching some 40,000 sermons in order to spread 'scripture holiness throughout the land'. He actually remained loyal to the established Church, in spite of its rejection of his ministry, for Methodism did not become a separate denomination until after his death.

Evangelical & Catholic

We should not use this term 'evangelical' in any party sense, for not only in the influences upon John Wesley before his conversion, but increasingly throughout his ministry, the classical writings of the wider Church, both East and West, informed and sustained him:

He read avidly the classics of spirituality: the early Fathers of East and West, Basil, Chrysostom, Augustine and Jerome. He valued Ephrem Syrus and Macarius the Egyptian (a disciple of Gregory of Nyssa)[4] and a whole wealth of Catholic writers in the area of spirituality and holiness.

THE FLAME OF SACRED LOVE

The term 'evangelical conversion' may be used of Antony of Egypt (c.251–c.356), when, at twenty years of age, he heard the Gospel reading: 'If you wish to be perfect, go, sell your possession, and give the money to the poor, and you will have treasure in heaven; then come, follow me' (Matthew 19:21). He did just that—gave away his inheritance and went into the desert to live the life of prayer with an amazing hermit ministry. His response to a young monk about a rule of life was:

> *Wherever you go, have God always before your eyes; in whatever you do or say, have an example from holy scriptures; and whatever place in which you dwell, do not be quick to move elsewhere. Keep these three things and you will live.*[5]

The story of Antony's conversion was the very one which Augustine (345–50) heard from his friends Ponticianus and Alypius, in Milan, when he was at a crisis moment in his life. He had spent his years in philosophical and religious study, alongside a moral laxity in which his attitude was 'give me chastity and continence, but not yet'.

In a very moving account in the *Confessions*, Augustine left his friends and threw himself down in tears under a fig tree in the garden. Suddenly he heard a child's voice singing, as in a game: '*tolle lege, tolle lege*'—'take it and read, take it and read'. He took up the book of Paul's letters and opened it to startling words:

> *Let us live honourably as in the day, not in revelling and drunkenness, not in debauchery and licentiousness, not in quarrelling and jealousy. Instead, put on the Lord Jesus Christ, and make no provision for the flesh, to gratify its desires.* (Romans 13:13–14)

This was a crisis moment—a shaft of judgment and illumination by the Holy Spirit. With the command to conversion and holiness in that moment, there came to Augustine both the will and the ability to make the break with sin, and open his life to Christ:

> *I had no wish to read more and no need to do so. For in an instant, as I came to the end of the sentence, it was as though the light of confidence flooded my heart and all the darkness of doubt was dispelled.*[6]

The two words for conversion in the New Testament are *metanoia* and *epistrophe*. The first emphasizes the turning from the old ways of sin and selfishness and is usually translated 'repentance'. The second emphasizes turning towards God in a positive act of surrender. They come together in Peter's sermon to a gathering of people before the temple after the day of Pentecost. Following the proclamation of Jesus as crucified and risen messiah, he urges the people: 'Repent [*metanao*] therefore, and turn to God [*epistrephe*] so that your sins may be wiped out' (Acts 3:19).

Jesus' gospel use of the word is appropriately linked to the new life of childhood when he says: 'Except ye be converted, and become as little children, ye shall not enter the kingdom of heaven' (Matthew 18:3, KJV).

Conversion can be thought of as the response to the Holy Spirit's movement within us, and though it may seem like a purely human act of changing our mind and turning our will toward God, it is actually the human response to the inward work of the Spirit, leading to saving faith in Christ. It does not stop there, for there is a continuing life of conversion in which the Holy Spirit never ceases the work of sanctification and holiness, remaking the image of God within us.

CATHOLIC SPIRITUALITY

Catholic & Evangelical

John Wesley wrote a remarkable open 'Letter to a Roman Catholic' in 1749. Catholics frequently attended his preaching services in Dublin, and his letter is remarkably eirenical. He obviously felt that differences could and ought to be shared within a community of faith and love, rather than in a situation of estrangement and conflict.[1]

It is a small essay in ecumenical theology, and shows what he meant by the term 'catholic spirit' in his attitude. After laying out fifteen points of shared common belief, he writes:

> *Are we not thus far agreed? Let us thank God for this, and receive it as a fresh token of his love. But if God still loveth us, we ought also to love one another. We ought, without this endless jangling about opinions, to provoke one another to love and to good works. Let the points wherein we differ stand aside: here are enough wherein we agree, enough to be the ground of every Christian temper and of every Christian action… Then if we cannot as yet think alike in all things, at least we may love alike. Herein we cannot possibly do amiss. For of one point none can doubt a moment: God is Love; and he that dwelleth in love dwelleth in God, and God in him (1 John 4:16).*

Here is evidence, in the warring days of religious conflict in Britain and Ireland in 1749–50, that the Wesley brothers had entered into an ongoing process of conversion which enabled them to be prophetic in their lives and preaching, and yet ecumenical in their attitude far in advance of their persecutors.

In our own day, though religion of an aggressive kind can be a source of conflict, division and violence, yet there is a new spirit of openness and sharing within the communion of the Church, and between people of reconciliation and peace in other faiths. If conversion is a manifestation of the Spirit of God, it must not produce an exclusivist mentality, and must not ally itself with political and violent forces to promote itself. Conversion is away from hatreds, divisions and sinfulness, towards the loving mercy of the reconciling God portrayed by the man on the cross whose arms are stretched out in forgiveness and reconciliation to all who will turn to him.

Conversio morum

Thinking about John Wesley's open 'Letter to the Roman Catholic', I was reminded of the conversion which has acted as the greatest spiritual catalyst to ecumenical spirituality in the last few decades. I refer to the conversion of Thomas Merton who wrote his story for millions to read in *The Seven Storey Mountain* in 1949.[2]

Over the years, he came to see that conversion was not only a moment, but a process, each stage containing in itself the fullness of the last. Merton saw his initial conversion taken up into the larger Benedictine vow of *conversio morum*, which means the conversion of the whole of life. He makes the matter clear:

> It is evident that the story of my life up to the day of my baptism is hardly the adequate story of my 'conversion'. My conversion is still going on. Conversion is something that is prolonged over a whole lifetime. Its progress leads it over a succession of peaks and valleys but normally the ascent is continuous in the sense that each new valley is higher than the last one.[3]

During his twenty-seven years as a monk, Merton underwent many experiences of conversion in the larger context of *conversio morum*. He matured into a man whose heart became wide open to the whole world, having to unlearn, on the pilgrimage, many religious dogmas and practices that were taught him in his early pre-Vatican II monastic life. He became not only a man of paradox, but of seeming contradiction in the kind of religious and political world that is acceptable to establishment values. The matter is made explicit with deep feeling in a Letter from Gethsemani, which his fellow monk, Matthew Kelty, wrote on the day after Merton's funeral in 1968:

The readings from the book of Jonah in the mass were not inappropriate! There was the whale (the coffin) in front of us with Fr. Louis [Merton's monastic name] inside... I do not know how to summarize the man—the thought is not even decent!—except to say that he was a contradiction. He lived at the centre of the cross where the two arms meet. Maybe you could say at the heart of life. And my guess is that at no other place is contradiction reconciled. He was a problem to many, here also, and this is the reason for the problem: I mean the terrifying tensions the man endured with a kind of courage that only the power of God made possible. I kept feeling when close to him: God is near. And to be near God is to be near something at once wonderful and terrible. Like fire. It burns. People were forever trying to get out of the spot made for them (by his simply being what he was) by putting him into some category or other and then making him stay there: about as good as bottling fog! For the task was impossible. They would decide he is a 'monk' and this is what a monk should be. Then they would expect him to be that. And he wouldn't, couldn't? Or hermit? Very well, this is what a hermit is... And then they would see if he is being a good hermit. And he would not be!! And so on. In everything.[4]

His was the measure of genuine evangelical and catholic conversion. Another of the monks from Gethsemani (Merton's monastery in Kentucky, USA), John Eudes Bamberger, wrote of the quality of Merton's life and witness:

There was a steady stream of persons of multifarious interests coming to speak with him from all over the world. He counted among his friends Vietnamese Buddhists, Hindu monks, Japanese Zen-masters, Sufi mystics, professors of religion and mysticism from Jerusalem's university, French philosophers, artists and poets from Europe, South America and the States, Arabic scholars, Mexican sociologists and many others. He was not only at home with all these men, he was on most friendly terms with each, and anyone who has been at the informal meetings he held with them over the years recognized how much pleasure he took in such company.[5]

Compatible & essential

Conversion, in Merton's experience, was an evangelical experience. It included those elements of gospel life in which repentance for a sinful past and turning in faith to the crucified, risen Saviour were an integral part. It became increasingly catholic as it developed a spirituality of word and sacraments in which there was a transformation of the ethical life, so that the love of God shone through.

It was *conversio morum*, a turning of the whole of life to God. Not only personal life, but a participation in, and transformation of, the monastic ideal. In Merton's case there was a radical interpretation of the gospel in social and political terms, in which the kingdom of God became manifested in his prophetic words and actions. And because his life and writings were in the forefront of contemporary spirituality, he disturbed the comfort and complacency of both Church and state.[6]

There was no doubt the personal and corporate conversion represented in Merton's thinking in his harrowing essay on Adolf Eichmann, where he makes the point that a demonic power is unleashed when religion and politics go hand in hand to further their own ends. The generals and the fighters of both sides in the Second World War were the 'sane ones' who carried out the total destruction of entire cities. It is a devastating evaluation:

> *Those who have invented and developed atomic bombs, thermonuclear bombs, missiles; who have planned the strategy of the next war; who have evaluated the various possibilities of using bacterial and chemical agents: these are not the crazy people, they are the sane people. The ones who coolly estimate how many millions of victims can be considered expendable in a nuclear war, I presume they do all right with Rorschach ink blots too. On the other hand, you will probably find that the pacifists and the ban the bomb people are, quite seriously, just as we read in* Time, *a little crazy.*[7]

This continuing sense of conversion is a process we call sanctification. It means that we are converted each day from that way of thinking and living that is ego-centred and sinful, to the forgiving love of God and neighbour. The Holy Spirit is the motive and mainspring of such a process, and although it is deeply personal, it also has its social and corporate dimensions.

It is evangelical by reason of its basis in the good news of gospel faith and repentance, but it goes on to catholic expression in a corporate and sacramental faith rooted in the life of prayer. The words 'evangelical' and 'catholic' do not indicate a party spirit. They are integral to a wholesome spirituality and cannot afford to exist or remain apart. As I have written elsewhere:

> *The word 'evangelical' indicates the profoundly personal experience of God in Christ, in which the Holy Spirit initiates the powers of the new birth in the life of the repentant sinner. Warmth, enthusiasm, zeal and apostolic dedication are all marks of the true evangelical spirit, and faithfulness to the revelation of God in scripture is basic to the evangelical perspective.*
>
> *The word catholic denies none of this—indeed at best will affirm the doctrinal and experiential elements of biblical evangelicalism. But there are the added emphases which underline the corporate nature of the Church as the body of Christ, and an unfolding of the sacramental and mystical life of the Church in which the believer within the body is sanctified, in attendance to word and sacrament. There is also great attention given to the corporate and personal life of prayer as taught within the Church's mystical tradition.*[8]

If we emphasize the evangelical and neglect the catholic, then there is danger of dogmatic bigotry, and an exclusive spirit which refuses fellowship, disrupts the unity of grace and results in a proliferation of sects.

But if we emphasize the catholic and neglect the evangelical, then there is the danger of a kind of 'churchianity' developing, which tends towards outward formality, ritualism and idolatry, with a neglect of scripture and a mechanical attitude towards the sacraments.

There is only one Church of God, and it is a cause of great sadness that our denominational divisions do not reflect our one Lord, one faith and one baptism. But these are also ecumenical days, and that very word ecumenical means 'household' of faith. There is an increasing amount of sharing between the communions of Christ's Church, and wide-ranging consensus among theologians and liturgical practice. If I were to offer a retreat under the title 'A Christian Spirituality for Today', I would quite likely have among the retreatants (in alphabetical order!) Anglicans, Baptists, Brethren, Catholics, Methodists, New (House) Churches, Pentecostals, Quakers, Salvationists, URCs, and perhaps (because they are thinner on the ground) one or two Lutherans and Orthodox.

There is quite likely to be a Baptist wanting to make his confession, a Methodist fingering at the Jesus Prayer rope, a Quaker asking if she can share the eucharist and a Catholic and Methodist sharing the laying-on-of-hands and anointing of the sick.

I would like to feel that we are all looking towards Vincent of Lerins' famous formula of the basic content of the Christian faith: 'That which has been believed everywhere, always and by all'. He did not mean that to be a rigid or dogmatic definition because he goes on to affirm that 'there should be a great increase and vigorous progress in the individual as well as in the entire Church as the ages and the centuries march on, of understanding, knowledge and wisdom'.[9]

Within this ecumenical household of faith, many Christians live together, and they don't always agree in terms of Christian doctrine and practice—especially in the liturgical area. The latter often depends upon temperamental and aesthetic factors, rather than objective doctrinal and pastoral judgments. What I often find is that disagreements are not across denominational groupings, but within them. I see the Lord's sense of humour when I find a Baptist evangelical friend kneeling in devout prayer at Glasshampton, surrounded by clouds of incense at the service of benediction!

We all need a spiritual home, for we cannot be spiritual freelancers or vagrants, and few of us will be *completely* at home within our own communion, though it is the right place for us to be. I find in the Anglican communion a catholic, evangelical and ecumenical faith and practice which is alive and communicable. But a high cost is paid for its comprehensiveness and breadth, for it takes charity, tolerance and humour to contain the evangelical, the catholic and the liberal groups with their particular emphases, in creative tension. It enables me to affirm a strong evangelical faith in the context of catholic liturgy, church order and devotion, and it challenges me with intellectual and social dimensions which stretch me in all directions. But lest I sound as if I'm inviting the reader to become an Anglican, let me hasten to say that for me, the Anglican communion is 'the best of a bad lot'!

I have Christian friends in other communions who treasure particular aspects of doctrine and practice more fervently in a different mix to mine, and no one communion has a monopoly on the truth. Fortunately, there is a rich sharing and pooling of resources in these days, and in areas of biblical scholarship and social outreach ecumenical co-operation is essential.

Every Christian, in whatever part of the Church they find themselves, should have a burning desire that the unity of Christ's body should not only be affirmed, but experienced and manifested. The scripture (among others) to keep in mind and heart is the whole of the Ephesian epistle, expressed in the words:

> ...lead a life worthy of the calling to which you have been called, with all humility and gentleness, with patience, bearing with one another in love, making every effort to maintain the unity of the Spirit in the bond of peace. (Ephesians 4:1–3)

ROOTED IN SCRIPTURE

Scripture as the basis of spirituality

This morning, in my hut chapel, I turned up the first reading at morning prayer and discovered it was the story of the boy Samuel lying in the darkness of the temple at Shiloh when the word of God came to him in the solitude, and marked his life from that moment. Take your Bible at this point and read the text in 1 Samuel 3:1–10.

The effect of such a visitation of the divine word to Samuel is spelled out in verses 19–21:

> *As Samuel grew up, the Lord was with him and let none of his words fall to the ground. And all Israel from Dan to Beer-sheba knew that Samuel was a trustworthy prophet of the Lord. The Lord continued to appear at Shiloh, for the Lord revealed himself to Samuel at Shiloh by the word of the Lord.*

Because my childhood was so precious to me, rich in spiritual awareness before I experienced a saving knowledge of Christ, and because my life from twelve years of age was saturated with the Bible, I could not help lingering over this passage this morning, and then singing before God the hymn which appeals to me by its very childlikeness, immediacy and simplicity. Perhaps you should learn it by heart, as I have done, and sing it in the context of this chapter of scripture and prayer:

> *Hushed was the evening hymn,*
> *The temple courts were dark,*
> *The lamp was burning dim*
> *Before the sacred ark,*
> *When suddenly a voice divine*
> *Rang through the silence of the shrine.*

The old man, meek and mild,
The priest of Israel, slept;
His watch the temple child,
The little Levite kept;
And what from Eli's sense was sealed
The Lord to Hannah's son revealed.

O give me Samuel's ear,
The open ear, O Lord,
Alive and quick to hear
Each whisper of thy word;
Like him to answer at thy call,
And to obey thee first of all.

O give me Samuel's heart,
A lowly heart, that waits
Where in thy house thou art
Or watches at thy gates
By day and night—a heart that still
Moves at the breathing of thy will.

O give me Samuel's mind,
A sweet unmurmuring faith,
Obedient and resigned
To thee in life and death,
That I may read with childlike eyes
Truths that are hidden from the wise.[1]

There is an indissoluble link between scripture and Christian spirituality. In the story of the great saints through the ages, and in the contemplative path of the contemporary Christian, there is a rootedness in scripture. If we are rooted in the Bible then the fruit will be joy and compassion—though we must qualify that, by the right understanding and interpretation of the written word, as otherwise things can go terribly wrong. Charles Wesley makes the close link between scripture and the work of the Spirit:

Come, divine Interpreter,
Bring us eyes thy book to read,
Ears the mystic words to hear,
Words which did from thee proceed,
Words that endless bliss impart,
Kept in an obedient heart. [2]

The inspiration of scripture

The word inspiration is rare. It occurs only once in the New
Testament, though it is a powerful analogy and its implications are
found through the whole Bible. The basic text is in 2 Timothy
3:16:

> *All scripture is inspired* [theopneustos] *by God and is useful for*
> *teaching, for reproof, for correction, and for training in righteous-*
> *ness, so that everyone who belongs to God may be proficient,*
> *equipped for every good work.*

Literally, the word 'inspired', *theopneustos*, means 'God-breathed',
and it immediately brings to mind the picture of God breathing
into Adam the breath of life so that he became a living being
(Genesis 2:7). The breath of God is the Holy Spirit, for the
Hebrew word *ruach* and the Greek word *pneuma* both mean spirit,
wind or breath, in the Bible. This breath of God is universal,
breathing life and fertility throughout the natural order, sustaining
animate life in all sentient beings, and inspiring all that is creative,
good and true in human endeavour.

This Holy Spirit breathes in creation and redemption, moving
the sinner to repentance, communicating the powers of the new
birth, and inspiring the human heart at all levels, and especially
through the prophetic word of scripture.

There is both a warning and an assurance found in our second
key scripture, in 2 Peter 1:21:

> *...no prophecy of scripture is a matter of one's own interpretation,*
> *because no prophecy ever came by human will, but men and*
> *women moved by the Holy Spirit spoke from God.*

The Greek word for 'moved' in this text literally means being borne along, and it is used of the ship in which Paul travels in Acts 27:15. As a ship is borne along in the sea by the wind in its sails, so the prophet is driven by the inspiration of the Holy Spirit. That ensures that the prophet delivers divine revelation and not simply a private opinion or interpretation. Such an affirmation means that the Holy Spirit, who inspired scripture in the first place, is also at work in interpretation within the fellowship of the Church. The biblical writers were not passive recipients of a mechanistic process, for the inspiration and interpretation of scripture are not static but dynamic movements in the divine–human relationship.

No one communion of the Church of God holds a monopoly of the truth, but the Spirit interprets the written word for every age, while holding fast to the deposit of faith (1 Timothy 6:20; 2 Timothy 1:14). That is what we meant in the last chapter by quoting the 'canon of catholicity' of Vincent of Lerins, *'quod semper, quod ubique, quod ab omnibus'*—those things which have always and everywhere and by all have been believed.

By such a canon of judgment and interpretation we are saved, on the one hand from the private presuppositions and the prejudices of certain modern commentators who subject scripture to their own unbelieving and critical judgment, while on the other from the exclusivist and heretical sects which abound today, with their own dogmatic, private interpretations.

Therefore, the Church is not kept automatically from error by an infallible Church, council or book, but by the Holy Spirit who guards and guarantees the prayerful interpretation and communication of the gospel in every age. I have recently been working with the excellent two-volume commentary on the Gospel of John by the Roman Catholic scholar Raymond Brown, and have just greeted his newly published *Introduction to the New Testament* with great joy.[3] These volumes are an ecumenical, eirenical and scholarly venture, presented with academic integrity and devotional warmth, communicating the findings of biblical scholars across the denominational board. One of the most intriguing factors is that his areas of agreement/disagreement are not only presented fairly and objectively, but they run across the denominational loyalties and affiliations.

The inward testimony of the Spirit

Some words are very precious to me, but they contain a hidden danger. They are: 'Scripture is inspired because it is inspiring'. There is an element of subjectivity involved, and it has to be safeguarded by an understanding of objective inspiration. The Church did not confer authority or inspiration upon scripture, but simply recognized its inherent authority. After all, the Church existed before the New Testament, and its scripture was a product of the believing community.

The recognition of the inherent authority of scripture is demonstrated in the process of sifting and collecting the measured canon. But affirming an objective authority to scripture is of little use unless it is accepted as living and dynamic truth within the experience of the community. There must be corporate and personal self-authentication in the dynamic experience of the Church. We have just referred to the work of a contemporary Roman Catholic exegete in whose work the objective authority and subjective inspiration of scripture is an ongoing experiential task. As a statement of the inward self-authentication of scripture in the living experience of the Christian and the Church there is a classical paragraph at the beginning of John Calvin's *Institutes of the Christian Religion*:

> *Those whom the Holy Spirit has inwardly taught truly rest upon scripture, and that scripture indeed is self-authenticated; hence it is not right to subject it to proof and reasoning. And the certainty it deserves with us it attains by the testimony of the Spirit. For even if it wins reverence for itself by its own majesty, it seriously affects us only when it is sealed upon our hearts through the Spirit.*

My own experience as parish priest, pastor, evangelist, teacher, university chaplain, retreat conductor, friar—and even hermit— has constantly made me aware of my profound debt to biblical scholars of all denominations, and has confirmed in me, my colleagues and hearers, the truth of the inspiration of scripture. Scripture has always been, for me, the primary and supreme authority in matters of faith and conduct.

I find myself in sympathy with the stance of the great Anglican divine Richard Hooker in what he called 'multiform authority'. This was his classic synthesis of scripture, tradition and reason, with the Holy Spirit moving through each, though the primacy is given to scripture.

This primacy is basic, for it acknowledges the supreme importance of biblical authority in the Church and in the believer's doctrinal, devotional and ethical life. It also implies that it is God who alone bears infallible authority, and that he reveals himself in scripture, in the dynamic tradition of the Church's experience, and values the human mind in the understanding of the way in which his will and character is mediated.

Hooker's multiform authority works with the three sources of scripture, tradition and reason. A contemporary theologian, John Macquarrie, prefers to use the term 'formative factors' in theology, and he lists them:

experience

revelation

scripture

tradition

culture

reason [4]

He makes the point that revelation is the primary source of theology, and a basic category in theological thinking. For him, scripture is a record of what he calls 'primordial revelation', and it gives the community access to such revelation. Bearing in mind God's revelation to Moses as a primordial revelation at the burning bush, recorded in Exodus 3:1–15, he lays out a basic pattern of revelation which may be the basis for a later scripture record:

The basic pattern may be summarily analyzed as follows: a mood of meditation or preoccupation; the sudden in-breaking of the holy presence, often symbolized in terms of the shining of a light; a mood of self-abasement (sometimes terror, sometimes consciousness of sin, sometimes even doubts of the reality of the experience) in face of the holy; a more definite disclosure of the holy, perhaps

the disclosure of a name or of a purpose or a truth of some kind
(this element may be called the 'content' of the revelation); the
sense of being called or commissioned by the holy to a definite task
or way of life.[5]

Such a written account provides a memory for the community by which it can recall and relive the past, just as the brain provides storage cells on which the memory of the individual depends.

So inspiration works in that the primordial revelation is an objective and immediate narrative of confrontation with God, and it comes alive as the scriptural record is remembered and relived in the community gathered around the word. This pattern gives an objective stability to the community, and delivers it from subjective heresies:

Scripture, as bringing again the disclosure given in the primordial
revelation, has a stability and even a kind of objectivity as over
against the vagaries of individual experiences in the community.
The scriptures of a community are a major factor in maintaining
stability and a sense of continuing identity in the community itself.
We find therefore that scriptures become a norm in the theology
of the community, and along with tradition provide a safe-
guard against the subjectivist excesses that arise from placing too
much emphasis on the deliverances of present experience. In the
Christian community, any theology which claims to be Christian
theology (as distinct from someone's private philosophy of religion)
must maintain close and positive relations with the Bible.[6]

The interpretation of scripture

We have drawn attention to the danger of private interpretation and the necessity to 'think with the Church' in an historical and contemporary understanding of the Bible teaching. In the course of the Church's history there have been over-literal interpretations of scripture and gross allegorization to the point of absurdity. Exegesis (reading *out* of the text) is the proper, disciplined interpretation of the meaning of particular passages or books of the Bible in their proper context, and their application for today. When a person or group uses methods of allegorical interpretation which make any passage teach what they subjectively want it to teach, then such abuse has been called *eisegesis* (reading *into* the text)[7] Augustine has a useful couplet which may be freely translated:

In Vetere Novum latet
et in Novo Vetus patet

The New is in the Old concealed
The Old is in the New revealed.

In the Middle Ages, the standard method of Bible interpretation was known as the *Quadriga* or the fourfold sense of scripture. In addition to the literal sense, three other senses could be distinguished:

The literal sense, to be taken at face value;

The allegorical sense, in which the Old Testament may contain 'types' or foreshadowings of Christ, or passages which were too obscure or unacceptable to be taken literally or at face value;

The moral sense, which interpreted passages as principles for ethical guidance;

The anagogical sense, which interpreted passages prophetically, pointing towards ultimate future fulfilment in the new Jerusalem of heaven.

Some such method acknowledges the literal sense as basic, but gives plenty of leeway for accommodation and interpretation in which the Church or the believer is not tied to a fundamentalist interpretation. The danger of the latter is that scriptural authority may be cited for violence, bloodshed, holy wars, apartheid and discrimination of every kind. It is salutary to note that nearly all the heretical sects affirm a plenary inspiration of the Bible while denying the divinity of Christ, and therefore the incarnation and the Holy Trinity. The Jehovah's Witnesses are a case in point, though this does not deny the sincerity and moral integrity of members of the sect.

If I were to select a typical biblical teacher who has the communicative common touch and has been the means of interpreting scripture to many thousands in all parts of the Church, it would be William Barclay. In his biography he has a marvellous teaching paragraph which communicates a great deal of biblical truth in a small space, and it illustrates the test of interpretation that I am concerned with:

> There are four Greek words for four different kind of preaching. There is kerugma. Kerugma means a herald's proclamation, and it is the announcement without argument of that which is most surely believed. It is the plain, uncompromising statement of Christian belief. There is didache. Didache means teaching. Suppose someone says 'so what?' If we can tell them 'so what', the meaning and the relevance of the kerugma as stated, that is teaching. There is paraklesis. Paraklesis means exhortation, and it is the appeal to the hearers to accept and act upon what the teaching has laid down. There is homilia. Homilia is the treatment of any subject in the light of the Christian message. It may be not entirely true to say that a very great deal of modern preaching is paraklesis, exhortation, but it is entirely obvious that there is no point in exhorting people to be Christians until they know what being a Christian means. And this is to say that there is an urgent need for a return to a teaching ministry.[8]

The Holy Spirit as true interpreter

To draw the threads of this chapter together I want to return to Charles Wesley. He has an important hymn on the inspiration of scripture in which objective and subjective inspiration of the word and the believer are affirmed. It is one of those hymns which should be learned by heart, to repeat and sing as you enter into prayer and Bible study, because it produces a receptivity in which the Spirit can minister directly to the believing reader or group in the contemplative study of the Bible.

The hymn is Wesley's 'Come, Holy Ghost, our hearts inspire'.[9] The first verse is an invocation for the Holy Spirit to come with prophetic fire to produce holy warmth, and to light up the written word with the divine love. The second verse records the continuity between the inspiration of the prophets and recognizes that only the Spirit who inspired scripture can unlock the truth to us. The third verse calls to mind the image of the Spirit as the brooding dove who produced light, life and harmony out of the primeval chaos in Genesis 1:1–5, and calls upon the Spirit to act as powerfully upon our disordered natures.

The final verse is one of the high moments in Wesleyan hymnody, indicating that only God can communicate his own nature of love and light, and that in such communication there arises a sharing and celebration of the wonder and glory of God among his saints:

> Come, Holy Ghost, our hearts inspire,
> Let us thine influence prove;
> Source of the old prophetic fire,
> Fountain of life and love.
>
> Come, Holy Ghost, for moved by thee
> The prophets wrote and spoke,
> Unlock the truth, thyself the key,
> Unseal the sacred book.
>
> Expand thy wings, celestial Dove,
> Brood o'er our nature's night;
> On our disordered spirits move,
> And let there now be light.
>
> God through himself we then shall know,
> If thou within us shine;
> And sound, with all thy saints below,
> The depths of love divine.

A DISCIPLINED LIFE

The training of an athlete

The words 'discipline' and 'asceticism' are not very popular in our contemporary society and yet in the so-called 'real' world strange extremes are obvious. On the one hand there are men and women who are hyperactive, working their socks off for money and power, while at the other extreme there are people of all ages who seem to be unemployable, with nothing to do and with such a low self-esteem that they cannot use their leisure for anything creative or life-giving. And the gap between the two seems to be widening.

This chapter is an encouragement to the believer to integrate a basic simple discipline into life. The aim is to present a sane mind in a healthy body in dedication to the Lord, so that body, mind and spirit may be unified in loving service—and a sense of fulfilment and joy will follow.

The goal is not always possible, of course, but when we are faced with the problems of age, sickness and disability, we shall then have the interior resources not only to cope, but to find the presence and strength of God in the present moment. I write these words having spent the last nine years exploring the hermit life, with an emphasis upon a simple and disciplined life of joy, in which prayer, study and manual work have provided the context of a creative life and ministry.

But over the last six weeks or so I have been incapacitated by back and hip pain which has made me nearly immobile, stopped my digging, and left me with a garden full of growing vegetables surrounded by encroaching weeds, and scores of potted french beans and leeks which I haven't had the mobility to transplant to their waiting plots.

This period of immobility is, I hope, transient, and I am learning from it. But there are many Christians who have to face critical illness, depression or catastrophe which will not be temporary

—and they will need a spirituality which will meet those particular needs.

The value of a good and balanced discipline is that it channels the dynamic energy of youth and enthusiasm, and it imparts the intuitive wisdom to deal with life's inevitable problems. The apostle Paul held things in proper perspective when he thought of Christian discipline in terms of the spiritual athlete:

Surely you know that many runners take part in a race, but only one of them wins the prize. Run, then, in such a way as to win the prize. Every athlete in training submits to strict discipline, in order to be crowned with a wreath that will not last; but we do it for one that will last for ever. That is why I run straight for the finishing line; that is why I am like a boxer who does not waste his punches. I harden my body with blows and bring it under complete control, to keep myself from being disqualified after having called others to the contest. (1 Corinthians 9:24–27, GNB)

Discipline & spontaneity

Jesus was neither a stern ascetic, like John the Baptist, nor a religious teacher who did not practise the disciplines he preached. He bore a yoke of service and called others to take it up. But it was a yoke of fellowship, of lightness and joy. I have some friends whose religion is a bit of a burden, for they are somewhat buttoned-up in their dogmatic and practical life. That would not be *so* harmful, but part of their legalism is an attitude of condemnation of those who do not agree with their opinions or subscribe to the narrow perspective and life-style they demand.

I have other friends who are so liberal in their beliefs and ethical life-style that it is difficult to see the difference between them and those who have no firm faith and discipline in their lives.

Neither of these groups cease to be friends, but lively discussion is part of our friendship, and both groups stimulate my thinking and living. Spontaneity has always been part of my attitude and style. To be able to respond to people, to nature, to all the creative and life-giving aspects of human life is a necessity for me. To get involved in new thinking in the Church and in the world is imperative. But such spontaneity can only blossom and flourish if roots are sunk deep into the soil of discipline and a certain asceticism.

I've always thought of myself primarily as a spontaneous fellow, and when, some years ago, someone said to me, 'You are a bit of an ascetic, aren't you?' with a grin on his face, I responded with a certain incredulity. 'Me?' I replied. 'I would think that the opposite is the case!' He then said: 'Well you don't smoke; you don't use alcohol; you are a vegetarian and you live a life under vows.' I had to protest: 'But those things are part of a simplified, affirmative life. They set me free from dependence, and it gives me joy not to have to kill to eat.' But I thought of what he said, and realized that motivation is an important factor in whether we are life-affirming or life-denying. It is not a matter of 'thou shalt not', but the determination of the athlete involved in the arena of service and ministry.

Simply being human

It was Irenaeus who said that to be fully a Christian is to be fully alive, and when I come across a religious person who is humourless, legalistic and life-denying, then I realize why the life-giving warmth of real humanity cannot flow through him or her. The disciples found it difficult to understand how Jesus could so easily accept the mothers mentioned in Matthew 19:13–14, embracing the children in such wholesome blessing and joy, or could, as a religious teacher, have an intimate conversation with a Samaritan woman, breaking the taboos of gender, race and sexuality in his warm, open and frank dialogue which resulted in the salvation of body and spirit for her (John 4:1–30).

One of the wonderful things about throwing in one's lot with Francis of Assisi in the following of Jesus is that one of the marks of a Franciscan is gospel joy. Under the heading 'Francis rebukes a gloomy friar' we read:

> *Why are you making an outward display of grief and sorrow for your sin? This sorrow is between God and yourself alone. So pray him in his mercy to pardon you and restore to your soul the joy*

of his salvation, of which the guilt of your sins has deprived it.
Always do your best to be cheerful when you are with me and the
other brethren; it is not right for a servant of God to show a sad
and gloomy face to his brother or to anyone else.[1]

This does not mean, of course, that real sorrow and pain cannot be expressed. There is a place in soul friendship when you can open your mind and heart absolutely and completely to a sister or brother and be enfolded in such understanding compassion that it becomes a healing balm to body and soul. But this is not to wear your heart on your sleeve. You should be warm and human in relationships—sometimes in ecstasy, sometimes in profound sorrow, and all stages between, depending on the quality of relationship. It is a matter of being simply human, and a religion which does not enhance and deepen your humanity is suspect, for it leads to hypocrisy, and to the extremes of either legalistic self-righteousness or the loneliness of despair.

If discipline and spontaneity are in place, within the context of a wholesome and shared spirituality, then it is likely that the believer can respond to people and situations in just the right way. The channels of spiritual energy and compassion will be wide open, and the response will be the flowing of the Spirit of God through these channels. I can reach behind the catholic/charismatic/evangelical divide if I quote a beautiful illustration of this from the life of the medieval mystic, John Ruysbroeck. See how free and spontaneous is his attitude. He is a man in love with God, and therefore wide open to all that is loving and human:

Spiritual inebriation is this; that a man receives more sensible joy
and sweetness than his heart can either contain or desire.
Spiritual inebriation brings forth many strange gestures in men.
It makes some sing and praise God because of their fullness of joy,
and some weep with great tears because of their sweetness of
heart. It makes one restless in all his limbs, so that he must run
and jump and dance; and so excites another that he must gestic-
ulate and clap his hands. Another cries out with a loud voice, and
so shows for the plenitude he feels within; another must be silent
and melt away, because of the rapture which he feels in all his

sense. At times he thinks that all the world must feel what he feels; at times he thinks that none can taste what he has attained. Often he thinks that he never could, or ever shall, lose this well-being; at times he wonders why all men do not become God-desiring.[2]

One of our postulants (the pre-novice stage) once told me of an experience he had with his adopted younger brother. The boy was depressed and miserable because he felt that being adopted he was not really part of the family (there were five children). Nothing his older brother could say could shake him out of his depression or persuade him that he was loved and appreciated at the heart of the family.

Suddenly, his older brother grabbed him, punched him playfully in his ribs, and wrestled him to the ground. At first he was passive and did not respond, but his brother, chuckling and playful, turned it into a game, and soon they were rolling around and laughing together.

That was the right action, at the right time, and it redeemed the situation, and brought the whole of the older brother's humanity to bear upon the younger boy's despair. And it worked. Of course it was risky, it needed discernment, it could have worsened the situation in other circumstances. But this is what a person in touch with his or her own humanity can do, and it is actually the *dynamis* or *energia* (the two Greek words for power and energy) which the Holy Spirit can accomplish in a dedicated Christian whose faith is positive and life-affirming.

Getting it together

There is a basic discipline for all Christians, and that involves regular attendance upon the word and sacrament in worship. The listening to the reading and exposition of scripture, the regular receiving of Holy Communion and the warm fellowship of a believing community is essential for a fruitful Christian life. But this is only the beginning. The individual Christian must work out his or her own particular life pattern, and as a member of a prayer or study group, while taking a clear stand on social issues which may involve peace, justice and ecological concerns.

The four major organizations in the publication of daily Bible notes have recently put their resources together to produce a sample booklet of a month's Bible readings under the heading *Grow with the Bible*.[3] They are:

BRF (The Bible Reading Fellowship)

CWR (Crusade for World Revival)

IBRA (International Bible Reading Association)

SU (Scripture Union)

I have been involved in the writing of the BRF notes, and it is an immense joy and excitement to be part of such a wide-ranging scheme, which is currently being distributed to churches of all denominations. The hope is not only that this will promote personal daily Bible reading, but encourage group reading, fellowship and action.

Christians often find that when they link up with movements which appeal to them, such as CAFOD, TEAR Fund, Amnesty International or a particular missionary society, it channels talents, time, energy and money, and provides them with the discipline needed to undergird their Christian discipleship. And for many this is sufficient, together with their basic church allegiance.

But these are ways in which Christians are seeking a deeper fellowship and spirituality, so that their experience of God is alive to what the Lord is requiring of them in their own pilgrimage and in the contemporary world.

One of the ways of doing this is by taking on a simple rule of life, with its roots in the gospel, and associated with tertiary or oblate membership with a religious order. To make this clear I shall describe what that means within the Society of St Francis, though a similar provision holds for the Benedictine or other orders.[4]

The Franciscan Third Order (SSF)

The First Order of Friars and the Second Order of Poor Clares already existed in 1216 when Francis preached at Cannara, and so many people wanted to leave their homes to follow Christ that he initiated what became the Third Order of Franciscans (tertiaries) which received canonical status in 1221 in Florence.[5]

There are many thousands of people throughout the world who are members of the Third Order of St Francis in the Roman Catholic communion, and a lesser number who belong to the Third Order of the (Anglican) Society of St Francis. There are other Franciscan groups and communities in other denominations. I write about SSF because it is the order to which I belong.

Francis of Assisi was not interested in promoting monasticism, but to lead people into a deeper love and discipleship of Jesus, and anything which deflects from that primary goal must be discarded. The SSF is a body of Christians which seeks to live out the gospel in the light of Francis. The framework and disciplines of a rule of life based on the gospel combine discipline and spontaneity, enabling the believer to make the ancient gospel contemporary in daily life. People who belong to the Third Order may be ordained or lay, women or men, and may be anyone from Bishop Desmond Tutu to a bricklayer, teacher, nurse or unemployed member of your congregation.

Aspirants, when accepted, would undergo a postulancy of around six months, leading to the two-year noviciate, and that leads to profession, at which tertiaries commit themselves to Christ within the order with lifelong intention.

A counsellor or spiritual director is assigned to help towards the mature realization of spiritual potential, and every tertiary draws up a personal rule of life with the help of his or her director. The rule affirms the gospel values of poverty, chastity and obedience, adapted for life in the world, in areas of prayer, study and manual work, and sounds the Franciscan notes of humility, love and joy.

Members of the Third Order pledge the rule for a year, and then renew it at the annual tertiary meeting. This renewed pledge is the basis of membership and the bond that unites members of the order. It is also a safeguard against merely nominal membership and promotes fellowship and love. This provides a dynamic sense of progression within the stability of rule and renewal.

The rule of life

The Holy Spirit is our true spiritual director, but within the body of Christ, spiritual care, confession and healing are among the charisms of the Spirit. A typical rule of life may run along these lines:

The holy eucharist. You should aim to receive the sacrament on Sundays and the greater festivals, and hope to include a weekly eucharist if possible.

Regular self-examination and meetings with your counsellor are commended, which may be followed by sacramental confession (at least before Christmas, Easter and Pentecost), or personal discussion seeking counsel and advice.

Prayer and meditation. Definite daily periods should be set aside for the daily office, and an evolving discipline of meditation under guidance. The minimum time may be stated, so that it can be kept without strain.

Life-style. Simplicity is the aim. There will be variation depending upon the age, outlook and temperament of the tertiary. It should include some physical exercise, commitment to study, and spiritual awareness. Matters of fasting, diet, disciplines of tobacco and alcohol, and the use of money are all involved, as are 'works of mercy' such as visiting the sick, lonely or imprisoned, and financial help to individuals or a chosen healing/reconciling agency.

Retreat. Tertiaries should make an annual retreat. It may be a Third Order retreat, or a group or private one. If for family or health reasons this is not possible, then a number of quiet days should be arranged.

Study. This is mentioned under lifestyle, but separate attention should be given to it depending on capacity and time. Bible study comes first, with commentary aids. It is worth taking advice, reading reviews and sharing in group discussion.

Study also involves learning a little about all the great human disciplines to broaden and deepen your understanding of God's world.

Simplicity. Again, separate mention is needed. In early Franciscan life, the distribution of your goods was a primary act, but of course this is relative to your family responsibilities. Sharing of what is retained should be kept in mind, involving hospitality, provision of transport if you have a car, and going back to your bicycle!

Work. If you have employment, be thankful! But quite apart from asking if your work is compatible with your Christian profession, it is necessary to allow the gospel to be expressed in daily work through attitudes, punctuality, honesty and open-hearted humour.

Obedience. Seeing your counsellor twice a year should be a matter of obedience. Consideration of obedience involves humility, trust, discipline and humour, and you should reflect on the obedience owed to love. Such reflection will also indicate your attitude to authority, responsibility and spontaneity, and be a fruitful area for self-evaluation.

Fellowship. As a tertiary, it is presumed that worship in your local church and fellowship with other Franciscans is part of your ongoing Christian life. Contact and fellowship with wider groups and other faiths are also encouraged, to keep open human channels of communication at every level.

Social dimension. Issues of peace, justice and ecological concerns will come with your way within the Franciscan family. Think these through and don't dissipate your energies.

It is better not to aim too high, for failing can lead to discouragement and unnecessary guilt—and that is certainly not what it is all about. It is better to set your sights lower than your expectation. Then a rule of life can be a help and guide, and can be adjusted according to changing circumstances.

The lover & the beloved

This chapter has been concerned with a disciplined life, but there is no rule other than love, and it is within the context of the discipline as lover and God as the beloved that our lives should be lived. Then rules disappear.

I love the story told by my namesake, Ramon Lull (the thirteenth-century Franciscan missionary and hermit), where he describes the lover wandering into a monastic cloister. The monks ask if he is a religious. 'Yes,' he answers, 'of the Order of my beloved.'

They enquire what rule he follows. 'The rule of my beloved,' he replies. Then he is asked to whom he is vowed. 'To my beloved,' he says. The monks then ask if he follows his own will. 'No,' he says again, 'it is given to my beloved.'

The lover is joined to Christ alone, and will not follow any monastic name, founder or rule. So he turns to the monks and asks them: 'Why do you who are religious not take the Name of my beloved? May it not be that, as you bear the name of another, your love may grow less, and that, hearing the voice of another, you may not catch the voice of my beloved?'

I have made the point. We need helps, guides, rules along the way, and we need discipline so that spontaneity may flow. But we shall see that there is a mystical path, described in the following chapters, which calls us into the deeper life of prayer and of the Spirit, in which we may so be indwelt by the Holy Spirit that the life of Jesus will flow in joy and compassion as we identify with the crucified and risen Christ (Galatians 2:20).

It is time to talk about prayer.

THE ADVENTURE
OF PRAYER

The river of prayer

One of the great joys in writing for the Bible Reading Fellowship is the appreciation of the reader's response. There was a particular feedback from recent notes in which I used the beautiful image of the river of God in Ezekiel 47:1–12 as a picture of the deepening life of prayer:

> *Going eastward, the man measured ten thousand cubits, and then led me through the water and it was ankle-deep. Again he measured one thousand, and led me through the water; and it was knee-deep. Again he measured one thousand, and let me through the water; and it was up to the waist. Again he measured one thousand, and it was a river that I could not cross for the water had risen; it was deep enough to swim in, a river that could not be crossed.*

The river flows from the altar of God in the temple, ever deepening as it flows, sweetening and purifying the salt wastes of Arabah. As it flows, fresh water fish appear, and the trees on either side of the bank begin to bear leaves and fruit for the healing of the nations. This image is taken up in Revelation 22:1–2, where the river of life, with the healing tree, manifests the glory of the kingdom of God, where all sickness and evil are healed and God dwells in the midst of his people.

In the Bible Reading Fellowship notes I used the image to illustrate the deepening life of prayer, for the prophet Ezekiel was invited to participate in the river's flow at different depths—ankle-deep, knee-deep, waist-deep and out of his depth.

I only leave my hermitage enclosure for two weeks of the year when I spend time with family and friends in Swansea, and it was during that time last year that I wrote the Bible notes, because I

THE FLAME OF SACRED LOVE

went swimming around the Gower coast. The following is the kind of thing I learned during that time:

Ankle-deep. This represents petitionary prayer—the first cry of need for forgiveness, for deliverance, for help in trouble or for strength in time of doubt or adversity. When Peter was sinking in the Sea of Galilee he cried out to Jesus: 'Lord, save me!' (Matthew 14:30). Experienced swimmers may venture far and deep, but they all have to begin at the shallows, ankle-deep. Here there is greater excitement, playfulness mixed with laughter and shouting as little children mingle with grannies and grandpas, paddling with skirts and trousers rolled up, accompanied by delighted screams as breakers roll in suddenly and catch them unprepared. Petitionary prayer includes all these elements of joy, hope, playfulness and surprise. You may only be ankle-deep in your life of prayer, feeling you've hardly begun, and yet even here on the edge of things the breakers roll in and carry messages from the great depths.

Knee-deep. This represents intercessory prayer. Progress into deeper water is gradual. From paddling to knee-deep wading is not a great distance but it is progress. Knee-deep is commitment, facing deeper water, from basic prayers of petition to greater awareness of others and concern for those who cannot pray for themselves—the beginning of intercessory prayer. Jesus leads us deeper. True intercessory prayer is not pleading with a reluctant deity to grant favours to an unworthy humanity, but rather a participation by that humanity in the healing energies of the Holy Spirit on behalf of sick and sinful men and women throughout the world. Wading knee-deep into the river of prayer is my response to the needs and joys of my friends and neighbours… and on into the deep waters of prayer for my enemies, and the beginnings of universal love.

Waist-deep. This represents the prayer of adoration. After playing for a while knee-deep in Langland Bay, I went floating on my back, out of the earshot of others, and began to sing:

O the deep, deep love of Jesus!
Vast, unmeasured, boundless, free;
Rolling as a mighty ocean
In its fullness over me.
Underneath me, all around me
Is the current of Thy love;
Leading onward, leading homeward,
To my glorious rest above.

Here are mingled prayers of thanksgiving and adoration, and I recalled the Celtic monks who used to sing the Psalter up to their chins in the sea. I rested in the Lord and allowed his love to flow around me. The border between waist-deep and waters to swim in is the place of adoration, and this may include thanksgiving, praise and the kind of 'tears-mingled-with-laughter' devotion that gives great joy to our Lord. It also leads to resting in his love—and I floated on the surface of the water, being sustained by the gentleness and power of the depths. Then, floating in those mid-depths, a fellow flashed past me, swimming a powerful underwater, overarm stroke, and soon disappeared away towards the sea's horizon. And I began to yearn for a stronger stroke, and for deeper depths…

Out of my depth. This represents contemplative prayer. Ezekiel calls it 'waters to swim in', and one experience last year made the point. Swimming in the bay in the early morning I went out too far, and on turning back found that the tide had also turned and was against me. After a breathless few minutes' hard swimming, I thought: 'I don't think I'm going to make it! Shall I end my life in drowning?' There were a few moments of quiet passivity, then I sent up some arrow prayers, and the resulting rush of adrenaline and effort eventually landed me back breathless on the beach. I have had a number of premature experiences of wading into the deeper waters of prayer over the years, and have sometimes found myself really scared, because I was both relatively unarmed against the powers of darkness (Ephesians 6:11), and relatively naked before the consuming fire of God's holiness and love. Only over the past few years have I begun to allow myself to be taken by the Spirit into those deeper waters. It is scary; it is overwhelming—but it is inevitable for those who are seeking the depths of God's loving mystery.

These levels of prayer are only a suggestive aid, of course. There are depths beyond depths in prayer, from the shallows to the mystery of the unplumbed ocean, answering to the mystery of God. In our experience, they mingle, and we do not outgrow the earlier levels. Even the profound saint or mystic will use simple petitionary prayer and engage in personal and communal intercessions. As to some of the contemplative depths, you will find more of those later in this book, but now let's note a few more things about the Ezekiel passage.

The vision of Ezekiel and its counterpart in the book of Revelation are of the same tree, its fruit and leaves for food and healing, fed by the river of God, which flows from his altar and throne. The river symbolizes the Holy Spirit flowing from the heart of God, made possible because the Son of God extended his arms of love upon the tree of life.

If we desire to enter that life of communion with God in the heavenly dimension beyond this mortal life, we must plunge into that river today. First, we must put our toes in to test the water, paddle ankle-deep, and then progress knee-deep, waist-deep, and so begin to swim as the Holy Spirit takes us deeper into prayer and into the mystery of God.

If we begin this adventure of prayer here and now, the effect will be gentle but radical, for the river deepens as we progress. First, there will take place the cleansing of our impurities in the water of God's grace, a deepening of our awareness of his loving action, an integration of all our physical and mental faculties as we learn to swim in his loving mystery. We shall experience the permanent indwelling of the Holy Spirit as we are surrounded, immersed and filled with prayer.

The result of all this will be a healing of the waters, life and fruitfulness everywhere, and a sharing of the healing leaves and fruit of the tree of life. All this is a preparation and foretaste of heavenly joy beyond this dimension of space and time. The deep waters are perilous as well as exhilarating—they are dangerous, as God is dangerous, but once you have begun there is no turning back. You know the experience of initial coldness when you first wade into the sea—but take the plunge; it is well worth it! The prayer at the conclusion of the Bible Reading Fellowship reading is one I would commend to you:

My Father, I believe the river of your love flows from your heart, through the world and into the dimension of eternity. Plunge me into that river, Lord, either gently and slowly, or by sudden and deep immersion, according to your will. Let me not be afraid, but bold in spirit, and make my life fruitful today and in eternity.

Holistic prayer

We shall later speak of the holistic nature of our salvation involving body, soul and spirit (1 Thessalonians 5:24). But here let us apply holistic thinking to the life of prayer. We have thought for too long that prayer was simply mental—we prayed with our brains! It is important for us to realize that we pray with our whole selves. We must allow our mind to descend into the heart; we must allow our human spirit to be possessed and indwelt by the Spirit of God. Only thus shall we enter into the dimensions of prayer.

A Basic Exercise

Let me take you through a basic exercise, a method of prayer on which you can build.

> *Posture.* Find a quiet place (chapel, room, garden or field). Wear loose clothing, remove shoes, and sit or kneel on a prayer stool, allowing your body to relax, with straight back and no tension.

> *Breathing.* Become aware of your breathing process, then slowly begin breathing from your diaphragm instead of from the top of your chest (belly breathing instead of chest

breathing). After some minutes, let your breathing relax to its normal rate, and simply rest in the presence of God, recalling that the breath of God is the Holy Spirit.

Meditation. At this point you may meditate upon scripture, repeat a simple Bible verse or word, or practise the Jesus Prayer.[1] But let me suggest a simple method that came to me via the Prison Phoenix Trust.[2] It is a Head/Heart exercise, and is illustrated below. Think of your breath in an L-shape: in through the heart; hold for a few seconds; then out through the top of the head. Then reverse the action: in through the top of the head all the way down to the heart; hold there for a few seconds; then out from the heart into the world. Study the illustration, and when you get the idea, simply practise it until you get the mechanics right.

IN   HOLD   OUT

IN   HOLD   OUT

This is a marvellous method of prayer and intercession which mingles the various levels of prayer, and can lead to the prayer of quiet in which you simply rest within the love of God, and allow him to transform your life.

At the first level of the illustration, you breathe through your heart, taking in the pain, suffering and sin of our world, holding it in love, and then breathing it up through your head, offering it to the healing grace of God.

At the second level of the illustration, you breathe in the healing power of the Holy Spirit through the top of your head, and down into your heart, holding it there in love, and then breathe it out to the needy world.

If you think of the Holy Spirit initiating and sustaining this method in and through your body, you will find that the whole of your being can be taken up into prayer. Once you have pondered this method you will find it so simple. It can be used wherever you are, waiting at a bus stop, in the doctor's surgery, as well as in the context of solitude and holy places.

Withdrawal. Withdrawal from a time of prayer and meditation should be gradual. You can once again become aware of your simple, relaxed breathing before the Lord, perhaps repeat the name of Jesus for a minute or two, and then gently say 'Glory to the Father, and to the Son, and to the Holy Spirit...' Then slowly bow, get up, stretch your limbs and get on with your daily routine.

The primary thing

Methods and techniques come and go. They suit some people, and are a hindrance to others. I have taught many basic methods of prayer and written about them,[3] and have practised the Jesus Prayer for over twenty-five years.

But the primary thing is to practise the presence of God. Sit before God in love, with his word in your hands and his peace in your heart. If your heart is toward him, he will do the rest. For prayer is nothing other than communion with God, though this may take many forms and manifest itself in various ways. It is simply the relationship of the believer in love with the Lord.

We shall be exploring many areas of prayer and spirituality in the following chapters, but through it all remember that Jesus said that only one thing is necessary, and that is to sit at his feet, and learn from his love (Luke 10:42). Charles Wesley puts it like this:

> *O that I could for ever sit*
> *With Mary at the Master's feet:*
> *Be this my happy choice;*
> *My only care, delight and bliss,*
> *My joy, my heaven on earth, be this,*
> *To hear the Bridegroom's voice.*[4]

TREMBLING

to its

SOURCE RETURN

There let it for Thy glory burn
With inextinguishable blaze,
And trembling to its source return
In humble prayer and fervent praise.

UNIVERSAL YEARNING

We have been thinking about the 'mean altar' of our hearts, upon which the sacred flame is ignited and sustained. It is right to begin with the human heart, for that is where we find ourselves. It is no use weaving a sophisticated metaphysical or scholastic pattern about the existence of God—as if God could be proved, or be found at the conclusion of an intellectual puzzle or scientific experiment. God is not 'an object among objects' to be proved or disproved, and that is why it is helpful for us to begin with the human heart, and we shall have much to say about its longing and restlessness.

But in this chapter, without moving away from our concern with human experience, our attention is directed towards the divine source which moves and stirs the human heart. That source is the profound mystery which causes the human mind to search for that which is beyond itself, and yet sensed and intuited in the depths of its own being. This mystery has always stirred humanity and initiated the quest for the divine, and up until the modern, secular world of the West, has been universal in its scope.

A useful phrase to describe it was coined by the philosopher Leibniz in the nineteenth century—The Perennial Philosophy[1]—though *what* he describes is something which was experienced and spoken of twenty-five centuries ago.

The Perennial Philosophy

First the phrase. It speaks of something which has always manifested itself wherever humankind had once satisfied its basic search for food, warmth and protection. The word 'philosophy' in this context is not an intellectual pursuit, but the love of wisdom, which is the word's real meaning. A study of the Perennial Philosophy is a lifetime's task, but in this chapter we shall lay out a basic broad definition, and understand it as the mystical soil in which all the major religions are rooted, and which is basic to any genuine spirituality, primitive or contemporary.

This way of moving into the origins of a genuine and vital spirituality may be new to the reader, but as I have introduced this way of understanding the soil in which our roots are firmly planted, I have found that it has been an exciting eye-opener to many committed Christians. A consideration of the mystical soil of our humanity, the fertile humus in which the seeds of religion and gospel can take root and germinate, is itself an experience of grace.

If this material is new to you, then let your mind and heart be stretched. You will begin to understand that this chapter is an appeal, not to the discursive intellect, nor yet to the unchecked emotions, but to that intuitive and discerning understanding from which the intellect and feelings flow. It is not itself revelation, but it is the source, the soil, the predisposition and receptive attitude in which revelation discloses itself.

The Perennial Philosophy makes four assertions and it rests on two fundamental convictions. Here they are:

The four assertions

They are not slick or simple, but they are basic and need thoughtful perusal, after which they will become clear:

1. This world of matter and individual consciousness is only a partial reality. It is the manifestation of a Divine Ground, in which all partial realities have their being. This is the basic and primitive way of saying that behind, below and within our created world is the life and mystery of God. However, we must not read later theologies into the assertion prematurely, but take it as it presents itself.

2. It is of the nature of human beings that they can 'know' this Divine Ground, first by inference, and second by intuition. This means, firstly, that a man or woman can contemplate the phenomena of the world, with its beauty, order, pattern, rhythm and regularity (e.g. the changing, regular, productive seasons), and infer that 'something is going on', and that something is the mystery of the creative life of the Divine Ground. It also means, secondly, that by the exercise of intuition, which is superior to intellectual reasoning, we can enter

into a certain knowledge, and a certain union with the Divine Ground.

3. The nature of our humanity is not single, but dual. We have two selves—our everyday, conscious ego, and also our somewhat hidden, true self which we may call our inner person, spirit or interior spark. This true self is of the same or like nature to the Divine Ground.

4. It is our chief end or goal to discover and identify ourselves with our true self. This involves an intuitive knowledge of the Divine Ground. Many images have been evoked to describe this process, for example, a new state of being, salvation, enlightenment, realization, new birth, eternal life, and so on.

The two convictions

As well as these four assertions, the Perennial Philosophy rests on two fundamental convictions:

1. Human beings possess an organ or faculty which is capable of discerning spiritual truth, though in most people it is atrophied and exists only potentially.

2. In order to be able to discern spiritual truth, we must become spiritual, participating in the divine nature. This involves a spiritual path of prayer, discipline, asceticism and compassion.

The soil for the gospel

The more we meditate on the Perennial Philosophy, the more it becomes clear how the gospel seed could germinate in such soil. The four assertions affirm that the mystery of God is behind, below and within all things, and that our material world and we ourselves are created by that reality. We arise from the Divine Ground of all that is. We are made by God and for God, and that is why the breath or Spirit of God which inspires all of us causes us to yearn for that Reality from which we all proceed. As Augustine said: 'You have made us for yourself, and our hearts are restless until they repose in you'.

But we cannot come to know God through our intellectual abilities alone. We have to descend from the mind into the heart—to an intuitive mode of 'knowing', in which the knower is united with the known in love. Our conscious, egocentric selves are distracted from the true, spiritual goal, and it is only as we discover that truer and deeper self that we can allow it to lead us to the source of our lives, which is God. For as John's Gospel says: 'This was the real light—the light that comes into the world and shines on all mankind' (John 1:9, GNB).

The meaning and goal of our lives must be to enter into a knowing and loving relationship with this Divine Ground of our being, or rather allow ourselves to be known and loved by the mystery of God. In the revelation of God in Christ, we come to know ourselves in the depths of our shame and glory, and enter into a loving knowledge of God. It is the Holy Spirit activating our human spirit that brings about this great miracle of the new birth, of enlightenment and salvation.

The Perennial Philosophy says that we have an organ or faculty which is capable of discerning spiritual truth. The reason why many would deny this, or are not conscious of it, is that it has become atrophied almost out of existence—and that is due to the fallenness of our human nature from the origin of our being. So, in order to be able to exercise this faculty or to use this spiritual organ, we must be cleansed, purified, disciplined. By prayer and compassion we must travel the spiritual path which leads to truth in love—the divine Spirit being our guide.

I have found many people in these secular days whose minds and hearts are closed to religious or 'gospel' truth, but if you share with them the source-wisdom found in the Perennial Philosophy, it plants their feet on a spiritual path which brings them into a new dimension of awareness and mystery—and that is but another name for God!

Some years ago I attended the annual meeting of Scottish Amnesty International in Perth. A group of humanist participants there assured me that they had fundamental and intellectual objections to God and religion. I asked them what kind of God they did not believe in, and when they explained to me their impression of the Church's image of God, I told them that I did not believe in the God they did not believe in—and for similar reasons!

Then I went on to talk to them about the Perennial Philosophy and the mystical tradition—that sense of wonder, awe and mystery with which we are dealing in this section of our book. It became clear that in their compassionate service for Amnesty, they were not only serving a wider humanity, but searching for that mystery which they could not name. They certainly could not identify it with the image of God which they had found in the established churches.

Once we begin to ask deeper questions of heart and mind concerning this source of the divine fire, we enter into the dimensions of mystery and mysticism, so let us reflect a little more about that in our next chapter.

THE MYSTERY OF GOD

Tremendous & fascinating mystery

Thomas Merton warns us against thinking that we have had spiritual experiences simply because we have read about them in books! This is a real danger with certain kinds of people. But there are times when we come across a piece of descriptive writing and we can say: 'Ah-ha! That is *just* what I have encountered, and I've never found it described or related with such immediacy and reality before!'

One of these experiences came my way when years ago I came across Rudolf Otto's *The Idea of the Holy*.[1] He wrote of that 'moment' in human experience in which a person encounters 'the holy'—he names it 'the numinous'. He does not indicate a rational or moral sense of righteous-holy, but of the numinous in which the soul is overwhelmed—that 'ineffable something' which makes our hair stand on end, causes profound fear and trembling within the presence of the divine.

He describes the 'creature feeling' which we all experience at some point in our mortality and finitude—perhaps a particular experience of deprivation, sickness, sadness or loss, or simply being alone in a world of other beings. Then he writes, that moment in which we may be grasped, touched, moved and stirred by what he calls *Mysterium Tremendum et Fascinans*—the overwhelming and fascinating Mystery, which is Being Itself.

This phrase caught up in itself the strands of experience which had intermittently invaded my life since childhood, causing strange joy and perplexity, and pointing towards a strange, promised hope of fulfilment which was beyond description or communication to others.

> *Mysterium* was that 'Other' which was not me and not other particular beings in the world. It was the word of depth, of presence which is all-pervading, breath-taking yet intermittently felt, and thus transient.

Tremendum indicated the awe-fulness, urgency and soul-shaking quality of the experience.

Fascinans indicated its drawing power, the unveiling which enabled me only to glimpse, but to glimpse with profound yearning, and to recognize that in spite of its Otherness, I was bound to It in the depths of my very being, and that It would give me no peace until I had entered into some kind of loving relationship—with all the fear that involved.

This was not a single, overwhelming experience—it came in fleeting moments, in certain moods, nearly always in solitude and especially in the context of earth, sea and sky.

These were periods before my twelfth year, and of course not only could I have not spoken in the language or images of Rudolph Otto, but I had no language to describe or communicate such experiences. In any case, it was intensely personal, and I felt in some childlike way that such experiences and emotions should be guarded.

I mention twelve years of age because that was when I entered into a simple but real evangelical conversion in which I made a personal surrender to Christ as Saviour, friend and brother. From that time I entered into the fellowship of the Church and began to interpret all my religious experience in the light of the Christian faith.

It was not until many years later that I read Otto's book, and began reading in the mystical tradition which I found in all the great religions. Then I discovered the specific Perennial Philosophy which we explored in the last chapter, which is the soil in which religion and revelation germinates and bears fruit.

I now continue in the mystical path of the Christian tradition, and believe that in union with Christ, which is the mystery of the Gospel (Colossians 1:26), is to be found the fulfilment of the pilgrim soul, of the Church of God, and of the entire cosmos which will be redeemed and transfigured ultimately in the kingdom of God.

We shall speak later about mystical experiences and moments of mystical vision which many people have, who would not dream of calling themselves mystics, but without defining the elusive

THE MYSTERY OF GOD

term Mysticism,[2] it would be helpful for us to have a simple and clear description which will serve our present purpose:

> In the true mystic there is an extension of normal consciousness, a release of latent powers and a widening of vision, so that aspects of truth unplumbed by the rational intellect are revealed to him. Both in feeling and thought he apprehends an immanence of the temporal in the eternal and the eternal in the temporal. In the religious mystics there is a direct experience of the presence of God. Though he may not be able to describe it in words, though he may not be able to demonstrate its validity, to the mystic his experience is fully and absolutely valid and is surrounded with complete certainty. He has been 'there'; he has 'seen'; he 'knows'. With Paul, in the poem by F.W.H. Myers, he can say:

> > Whoso has felt the spirit of the Highest
> > Cannot confound nor doubt him nor deny.
> > Yea with one voice, O world, though thou deniest,
> > Stand thou on that side, for on this am I.[3]

Universality of the mystery

The universality of the mystery of God is to affirm that the Holy Spirit has always been at work in our world, among all peoples and all times. Such a realization imparts a sense of freedom from an exclusivism which claims that only in the Church can any trace of God's saving power be found.

It is possible to hold that in Christ we recognize the unique Saviour of the world, and yet at the same time to believe that every person is touched by the indwelling *Logos* (John 1:1), and that the Holy Spirit is at work in the rhythms of nature, in all the creative arts and sciences, and wherever the revelation of God's love and grace are to be found—within and outside the specific Christian Church.

There are many reasons why, in our Western world, the tide of secularism has engulfed us. And though we may bewail the fact that the Bible is now little known, that the market philosophy has suffocated a sense of the sacred in our society, and that our culture is morally adrift, there are also benefits.

In our 'pick 'n' mix' society many people who would not dream of looking for a spirituality in the Church are willing to consider other possibilities. New-age religion is a mixed package, with some irrational and sometimes demonic ingredients. But among many seekers there is a new openness to the spiritual dimension, a new willingness to consider ancient spiritual paths.

A much-travelled friend recently told me that he has seen at airport bookstalls and in the hands of jet-travelling people paperback copies of the fourteenth-century mystical treatise *The Cloud of Unknowing*.[4]

When I spent my second six months of solitude on the edge of the Lleyn Peninsula during 1983–1984, two of the books I took with me were Fritjof Capra's *The Tao of Physics* and *The Turning Point*.[5] I was excited by the pilgrimage of this man who began as an agnostic. From his intellectual study of modern physics, he has travelled, via an initial mystical experience accompanied by tears, to an acknowledgment of the great spiritual and mystical traditions, and is now in dialogue with Christian monasticism.

It is worth recording the initial experience in which he sets the scene for his spiritual journey. This is the point from which he begins to relate his academic, scientific disciplines to the life-giving, mystical awareness:

Five years ago, I had a beautiful experience which set me on a road that has led to the writing of this book. I was sitting by the ocean one late summer afternoon, watching the waves rolling in and feeling the rhythm of my breathing, when I suddenly became aware of my whole environment as being engaged in a gigantic cosmic dance. Being a physicist, I knew that the sand, rocks, water and air around me were made of vibrating molecules and atoms, and that these consisted of particles which interacted with one another by creating and destroying other particles. I knew also that the earth's atmosphere was continually bombarded by showers of 'cosmic rays', particles of high energy undergoing multiple collisions as they penetrated the air. All this was familiar to me from my research in high-energy physics, but until that moment I had only experienced

it through graphs, diagrams and mathematical theories. As I sat
on that beach my former experiences came to life; I 'saw' cascades
of energy coming down from outer space, in which particles were
created and destroyed in rhythmic pulses; I 'saw' the atoms of the
elements and those of my body participating in this cosmic dance
of energy; I felt its rhythm and I 'heard' its sounds... [6]

We have spoken of this open and receptive attitude which is the prerequisite of revelation. Capra did not *seek* this insight, but was *open* to it. He did not demand it, impose himself upon it or discover it. It was unveiled to him—it just 'came to him', and he 'saw' and 'felt' and 'heard' and 'knew'. This was the end of the golden string—his research into physics—which led him to the unified structure of all things, and the cosmic dance manifesting the divine at the heart of all things. His latest book, *The Web of Life,* is subtitled 'A New Scientific Understanding of Living Systems',[7] and it continues the scientific and mystical quest with others from the scientific community who are involved in 'the new physics'.

Throughout the last three decades, a mystical theologian who has perceptively recorded his own spiritual journey, in parallel with his observation of what the universal Spirit is accomplishing across the world, is the Benedictine monk, Bede Griffiths.

Before his recent death he wrote *A New Vision of Reality,*[8] in which he shares his personal synthesis of Western science, Eastern mysticism and Christian faith. He says that we are at the end of an age which began three centuries ago with the discoveries of Galileo and Newton, resulting in the gradual development of a materialistic philosophy and a mechanistic model of the universe. The whole social, political and economic system of the West is governed by it. He agrees with Capra's *The Turning Point* in such an evaluation, and with him feels the beginnings of a new age in which people are turning from such secular reductionism, with a hunger for a spirituality to fill the vacuum in their lives. Here is part of his understanding:

In the second part of this [twentieth] century we have begun to
discover what has been taking place and in what we are involved,
and a new movement has begun which is the opposite of all this.

We are beginning now to be able to replace the mechanistic system and mechanistic model of the universe with an organic model. This is the beginning of a return to the traditional wisdom, the wisdom by which human beings have lived over thousands and thousands of years and with which the great societies of the past have been built up. In this ancient traditional wisdom the order of the universe is seen always to be three-fold, consisting not only of a physical dimension but also of a psychological and a spiritual world. The three worlds were always seen as interrelated and interdependent. This understanding of the three orders of being and of their interdependence is what is known as the Perennial Philosophy.[9]

Far from the restoration of this ancient spirituality being a drag on human life and progress, the opposite is true, for a new awareness of the mystery of God and of a contemplative vision is the only hope for our world. The matter is put succinctly:

At the present moment the whole movement of economics and politics is characterized and marred by the exploitation of nature at every level. The material resources of the universe are being grossly exploited in order to create more material prosperity for relatively few human beings, no matter at what cost that is done. That trend would be reversed by the new understanding that we are all part of this universe, of this natural world, that we are integral elements in it and that we have to respect it. This would involve a new attitude to the earth and to the natural resources of the earth, to the sea and all the creatures in it, to the animal world as a whole, to the question of vivisection and the treatment of animals in general, and to our attitude to outer space, whether we try to exploit it for human gain or whether we look on it in another way.[10]

It is as if we are being forced into an understanding of our human dilemma because of our own greed, selfishness and exploitation— what the Bible calls sin! We are becoming so hard pressed in our exploitation of the planet, the build-up of independent nuclear powers and our inability to live in international harmony that our spiritual bankruptcy is plain and obvious.

So the mystery of God is sounding again, prophetic voices are rising in surprising places and the ancient, traditional wisdom is presenting us with alternative ways of living in creativity and compassion.

The human heart is not satisfied by the material gains of our secular age, so we shall now turn to consider those moments of mystical or intuitive vision which many people experience, but few have been able or willing to share. The time for profounder mystical experiences and wider sharing has come.

THE TIMELESS MOMENT

The mystical touch of God

Many people think of mystics as an élite body of men and women who are far and away ahead of ordinary mortals in some spiritual dimension of glory and ecstasy. This is not so. Not only do the real mystics have their feet firmly planted on the earth, but they are immensely practical people, with hearts full of compassion.

Their deepest experience may be ineffable, indescribable, but they want to share it—indeed, it overflows from their lives of joy and fire. And the path is open to everyone, for it is in God's will that we should all find our feet planted on the way of penitence and illumination that leads at least to union with him in love. Though for most of us we only accomplish part of the journey in this life.

Having said that, this chapter is not about mystics, but about that touch of God which T.S. Eliot calls 'the timeless moment'. I want to draw attention to the fact that such an experience, transient and rare though it may be, is the experience of many, most, and potentially all people. Let me put it like this:

Everyone has the potential for this experience;

Many have unconsciously experienced it;

Many have secret experiences of it;

Some have acknowledged experiences of it;

Some have specific religious experience;

Some acknowledge it within the setting of a world faith.

The experience may not be mysticism as such, nor would the recipients call themselves mystics. That is why I use the term 'the touch of God'. The experience may be a glimpse, a moment, a transitory trembling, unexpected and unsought.

One of the most important things about such mystical touches is that they cannot be magically produced or manipulated. They are not under our power or at our beck and call. The initiative lies with the power that touches us, and there is a certain passivity on our part. That is why a receptive mood precedes the touch itself.

It may only happen once in a lifetime, or it may lead on to a mature spiritual life, in which the contemplative dimensions take priority. But when it does happen it brings an illumination and knowledge that cannot be accessed by rational thought, but which may change the whole direction of one's life.

Let's look at the categories I've mentioned:

Everyone has potential

In our chapter on the Perennial Philosophy, we said that human beings possess an organ or faculty which is capable of discerning spiritual truth, though in most people it is atrophied, and exists only potentially. This means that everyone is created for loving friendship with God and, simply by living, has experience of God. Either by spiritual neglect, or by giving themselves to material pursuit of gain, power, lust or evil, people do not realize this faculty for spiritual awareness. The more it is neglected, denied or mocked, the more it atrophies, though of no one should it be said that it completely dies in this life:

> Down in the human heart feelings lie buried,
> Feelings that only God's grace can restore;
> Touched by a loving hand, wakened by kindness
> Chords that were broken may vibrate once more.[1]

After a lifetime of crime, robbery and insurrection, the dying thief turned to Jesus on the cross, and was touched, moved and impelled to cry out: 'Jesus, remember me when you come into your kingdom'. And the Saviour was already waiting for him: 'Truly I tell you, today you will be with me in Paradise' (Luke 23:42, 43). There is a story that this thief once lay hidden behind some rocks when Jesus was teaching the people, and their eyes momentarily met as Jesus was saying: 'Come to me, all you that are weary and are carrying heavy burdens, and I will give you rest' (Matthew 11:28).

But be that as it may, even in his dying moments, the mystical touch of God moved the thief to enter the kingdom with his last breath. The point I make is that no one is outside grace, no one is disqualified, no one abandoned, save only as they finally, obdurately, purposely and stubbornly choose evil—in this life and when faced with eternal realities after death.

Many have unconsciously experienced it

I mentioned earlier some humanists who were working for Amnesty International, who had conscientious objection to what they had encountered in the Church and its image of God. Yet after our conversation I was able to show them that they had really experienced, in compassionate identification and idealistic service, the movement of the Holy Spirit in their lives. This was a new recognition—realization.

I only have opportunity for hitchhiking in my Franciscan habit once a year now, but I always prefer it to problematic public transport. On holiday one Sunday morning, I was travelling (without habit) from Swansea to Cardiff, and a fellow in his mid-twenties gave me a lift in his tatty van. As we drove along he asked me what my job was, and I suggested he guessed.

After he had mentioned teaching and social work, I admitted I was a friar! He was taken aback, and said: 'Oh, I'm not religious…'

'I'm not so sure,' I replied, and we went on talking, as he told me about his wide-ranging love of music and poetry, and then about his fiancée.

'But I'm not religious,' he repeated.

And I repeated: 'I'm not so sure!'

'What do you mean, you're not so sure?' he quizzed, looking at me from the corner of his eye.

'Well, you tell me that there are certain things which turn you on—which really move you. You love music, you read poetry, and I presume you would claim to be in love?'

'Yes, I think so,' he replied a bit sheepishly, but with a friendly grin.

'Those are the very reasons which indicate to me that you have been touched by the creativity, the joy and the love of God,' I told him. 'Anyone who has been deeply moved by any creative experience or discipline in the arts or sciences, and especially those who have experienced human love at any level have, by those very experiences, been touched by God.'

'And that makes me religious?' he asked.

'Yes, it means that such people have been touched by the creative Spirit, and they have themselves touched the edges of God's ways. Of course, it's only a beginning. There's a long way to go, but their experience is genuine and spiritual.'

'Tell me more,' he urged.

So I went on to speak of people of all ages throughout the world who have been touched, inspired and inflamed by the creative Spirit, who have been called seers, sages, gurus, prophets...

'Oh, like Isaiah,' he broke in.

'How do you know about Isaiah?' I asked.

He smiled and said: 'Well, I did go to Sunday School.'

'Ah, now your sins are coming out,' I joked, and I referred to some of the prophets who were seized by the Spirit and felt impelled to communicate their experience and message. And I went on to speak of the person of Jesus who was filled with the Holy Spirit and brought the revelation of God's compassion to a sick and needy world.

The conversation went on as the journey progressed, and it became a dialogue in which I related the positive experiences of his life to the providence, mercy and grace of the God who loved him, and whom he had experienced, albeit without realizing it. He was intrigued, asked more questions, and then he repeated: 'And that means that I am religious!'

We got to Cardiff, and before I jumped out of the van, he said: 'I've never met a fellow like you before...'

I looked him square in the eye and said: 'No, I don't suppose you have—but don't forget what we've shared.'

'No, I won't!' he replied. 'Maybe I'm religious!'

And we parted.

On the following Wednesday, I stood at Fforestfach Cross in Swansea, about fifty miles from where we had parted, hitching a lift to Llanwrtyd Wells. Suddenly, I heard a shout, and saw a fellow waving his arms. I went over to discover our friend, this time with a car and his girlfriend. 'Gosh,' he cried, 'this is the chap I've been telling you about. How is it possible that we've met again—maybe I'm religious!'

'Cool down!' I said, for he was so excited and the young woman said: 'Oh, he's been like this since Sunday...'

There is more to that story, but it serves to illustrate that this ordinary, friendly, warm-hearted fellow had experience of God, and when I enabled him to become aware of it, to have access to it, he was not only positive and intrigued by my evaluation, but became excited as he realized that 'something was going on'.

One of the great joys of my life has been simply to meet people where they are, take up the sources of wonder, creativity, compassion and human loving in their lives, and thereby help them to acknowledge that 'something is going on', and that if they will be open and receptive, then they will be drawn into a profounder interpretation of their human experience.

I don't try to impose an alien religion upon them, or start answering questions they've never asked—that is what turned them away in the first place. Michael Mayne puts it like this:

> So often Christians write as if they possess a privileged insight into what it is to be human and go on to speak a language that only the enlightened will understand. But if it is true (as I profoundly believe) that we are each made 'in the image of God', that we are bodies and we are also spirits, embodied spirits that have qualities not found in inanimate nature, then 'human' and 'Christian' are not mutually exclusive terms, nor is a Christian called to be anything other than human. Each of us is unique, yet the story of any one of us is in some measure the story of us all. What a Christian claims to have is a different frame of reference.[2]

Many have experience of it

Can you imagine the incredible joy of the young mother in being able to share the following experience with the Religious Experience Research Unit:

> The baby was put into my arms to suckle: as he attached himself to my breast and pulled on my nipple, my womb contracted strongly and I was flooded by a love of such intensity that it was

all-consuming; it enveloped myself, my child, and then seemed to extend beyond to the whole of creation. I literally felt no longer an individual but attached, a part of a large living whole… I felt in harmony with the workings of the cosmos, and it was indescribably beautiful. Over all this I felt I was within the radius of a 'presence', of something so great, so awesome, that I myself, small consciousness that I was, could only wonder but not fully comprehend.[3]

Many have acknowledged experience of it

Some twenty years ago Alister Hardy, the Oxford Professor of Zoology, founded the Religious Experience Research Unit at Oxford. He invited 'all who have conscious of, and perhaps influenced by, some power, whether they call it the power of God or not, to write a simple brief account of these feelings and their effects'. The Research Centre now has over 5,000 such accounts—many of which confess that they had not previously shared them, but were glad of the opportunity to do so. Whenever surveys of enquiry have taken place, the percentage of affirmative replies is always amazingly high. Two such polls initiated by the Research Centre in the 1970s and 1980s, elicited a 33 per cent and 62 per cent positive response.[4]

One of the childhood mystical experiences, at four or five years old, recalled fifty years later, is recorded by a woman who writes of a childhood walk over 'the moors' at Pangbourne, as the sun declined and a pearly mist formed over the ground, until she stood ankle-deep in gently swirling vapour:

Here and there just the very tallest harebells appeared above the mist. I had a great love of these exquisitely formed flowers, and stood lost in wonder at the sight. Suddenly I seemed to see the mist as a shimmering gossamer tissue and the harebells, appearing here and there, seemed to shine with a brilliant fire. Somehow I understood that this was the living tissue of life itself, in which that which we call consciousness was embedded, appearing here and there as a shining focus of energy in the more diffused whole. In that moment I knew that I had my own special place, as had all other things, animate and so-called inanimate, and that we were all part of this universal tissue which was both fragile yet immensely strong, and utterly good and beneficent.

The vision has never left me. It is as clear today as fifty years ago, and with it the same intense feeling of love of the world and the certainty of ultimate good. It gave me a strong, clear sense of identity which has withstood many vicissitudes, and an affinity with plants, birds, animals, even insects, and people too, which has often been commented upon. Moreover, the whole of this experience has ever since formed a kind of reservoir of strength fed from an unseen source, from which quite suddenly in the midst of the very darkest times a bubble of pure joy rises through it all, and I know that whatever the anguish there is some deep centre in my life which cannot be touched by it.[5]

Some have specific religious experience

Many of the experiences recorded within the files of the Religious Experience Research Unit came about within the context of nature, music, science or art, but many of them are directly related to specifically religious personages and themes. The woman who recorded the above nature-mysticism experience found it to be a continued source of life-giving awareness which conditioned her whole life and she goes on:

Years later, reading Traherne and Meister Eckhart and Francis of Assisi, I have cried aloud with surprise and joy, knowing myself to be in the company of others who had shared the same kind of experience and who had been able to set it down so marvellously.[6]

The following passage from children's author Rosemary Sutcliffe's autobiography should be placed side by side with the New Testament account of the transfiguration of Jesus. The religious text spills over to the transfiguration of the whole world, both in the present mystical experience of the believer, and in the kingdom which is to come:

The high-walled garden of Daniel's cottage was flickering in the coloured flame points of crocuses, white and purple and lilac and gold; each crocus opening to the sunlight seemed to me at once a star and a grail; a cup brimming with light. It is one of the mysteries, surely, this sense of light shining through rather than on; the whole world becomes faintly translucent and the light of the spirit shining through its substance, that comes with being in love. One has it as a child, but in childhood one knows nothing else and so is not conscious of it, till the heightened awareness is given back for this one time.[7]

Some acknowledge it within the setting of a world faith

One of the reasons why F.C. Happold's *Mysticism* is such a useful book is that he provides a series of essays on the nature of mysticism in the first part, and devotes the second part to an anthology of mystical experience in the Christian and other faiths.

One of his representatives is William Law, whose serious call to a devout and holy life so influenced the Wesley brothers. Here is a classic passage which is the fruit of Law's own contemplative vision:

Though God be everywhere present, yet He is only present to thee in the deepest and most central part of thy soul. Thy natural senses cannot possess God or unite thee to Him; nay, thy inward faculties of understanding, will, and memory can only reach after God, but cannot be the place of His habitation in thee. But there is a root or depth in thee from whence all these faculties come forth, as lines from a centre, or branches from the body of the tree. This depth is called the centre, the fund *or bottom of the soul. This depth is the unity, the eternity, I had almost said the infinity of thy soul; for it is so infinite that nothing can satisfy it or give it any rest but the infinity of God.*[8]

This chapter is really to encourage those who would never dream of claiming mystical vision to be willing to consider that those transient glimpses of glory that have invaded their ordinary and common lives may indeed be the ray of God's loving presence. Once this is thought possible, then an open and receptive attitude will lead to further and deeper disclosures of the love that lies at the heart of all things.

It may be a breakthrough of intuitive discovery, like Archimedes who suddenly cried out in his bath: 'Eureka! I have found it'—realizing that 'it' had found him! Or it may be in a glorious first hearing of Bach's great Toccata and Fugue in D Minor, which the scientist J.W.N. Sullivan called *the* cardinal experience of his life, a revelation—concerning which he wrote: 'I am quite unshakeable. I have heard, and I know.'[9]

It may happen during the quiet consideration of some great painting, reading of poetry, literature or the perusal of the spiritual journey of one of the great mystics.

From a child I have been moved to tears, laughter and exalted wonder by the earth, sea and sky. Even as I write from the quiet Sunday beauty of a midsummer day in my enclosure in the fields of Worcestershire I am caught away to a moment of childhood. I had spent hours getting to the outermost point of Worm's Head in the Gower Peninsula, and at last I stood beneath the great head of rock. Sky above, sea below, buffeted by wind and spray, I was 'gradually and suddenly' taken up into the glory of it all and cried out in wonder. How I would love to do that again before I die!

But I want to conclude this chapter on a much gentler note, recalling the transfiguration of the ordinary I referred to earlier, and recalling that it was in the opening buds of a tree in spring that was God's mystical moment for Brother Lawrence and which was the source of his vocation for a life of prayer in the Carmelite Order.

He never doubted that it was a mystical moment that changed his life. But in order for you to identify such moments in your own experience I want to point to a similar experience by Mark Rutherford in his journal which is simple, yet immediate and authentic:

One morning, when I was well over sixty, I was in a wood and something happened which was nothing less than a transformation of myself and the world. All my life I had been a lover of the country, and I had believed that the same thought, spirit, life, God which was in everything I beheld was also in me. But my creed had been taken from books... I was looking at a great, spreading, bursting oak. The first tinge from the greenish-yellow buds was just visible. It seemed to be no longer a tree apart from me. The enclosing barriers of consciousness were removed and the text came to my mind, 'Thou in me and I in thee'... The distinction between self and not-self was an illusion... I do not argue. I cannot explain. It will be easy to prove me absurd, but nothing can shake me.[10]

MYSTICAL & PROPHETIC RELIGION

Mystical & prophetic tension

Some years ago, when I was Guardian at our monastery at Glass-hampton, Richard (we'll call him), asked if he could join us for our meditation hour on Friday evenings, although, as he said, he was more of a Buddhist than a Christian.

I said that he could certainly join us, but that occasionally we devoted the first part of the hour to the Jesus Prayer. He was happy about that, and began to sit with us—a model of stillness during the hour leading up to Compline.

After some weeks he shared his story with me. His parents had been Protestant missionaries in India, and they kept their 'prophetic religion' intact from what they felt were the syncretistic religions of India. During his childhood and into young manhood Richard, while respecting his parents' faith, did not find it attractive, and the whole mystical dimension, which would have drawn him, was missing.

He lived in a theological college in Oxford during his secular degree studies, and found the same there—remembering the religious 'feel' of India, and the unsatisfied yearning of his own heart.

One day, waiting for a train, he saw a Buddhist monk on the platform, and approached him. 'Do you teach meditation?' he asked. 'And does one have to be a Buddhist in order to learn?' The monk assured him that if he was a Christian he could learn the methods and techniques of meditation while remaining loyal to his own faith. That was the beginning of Richard's pilgrimage, with an increasing appreciation of Buddhism, until some years later he arrived at Glasshampton, and our conversation.

He found the removing of sandals, the sitting cross-legged or on a prayer-stool, and the silence of the dim chapel a wonderful context for meditation, and realized that if he had found this dimension within his own Christian upbringing, things may have worked out differently.

I invited him to participate in a week's retreat I was due to conduct on the theme 'Mystical and Prophetic Religion'. He took it up, and for the first time in his life was confronted with the mystical dimension of the Christian faith.

Each session, I took a passage of scripture which illustrated both the mystical and prophetic elements of the mystery of God, and showed that an integrated Christian faith affirmed the transcendence of God in the prophetic tradition of Israel's prophets, within the context of mystical confrontation with the immanence of God in the *Mysterium Tremendum et Fascinans* we talked about under the heading 'The Mystery of God'. I carried this twofold understanding into the experience of Jesus and the apostolic teaching of the New Testament, and during the retreat we had silent meditation periods as well as the eucharist and liturgical worship.

Richard had never before entered into both the mystical and prophetic elements of the Christian faith, and it was not long before he was confirmed in his recovered faith, and during the years since has practised and taught meditation. He continues to be grateful to that monk he once met on the railway platform.

Spiritual pilgrimage

Some of the passages I dealt with in that retreat were:

Moses' confrontation with God at the burning bush
(Exodus 3:1–6)

Jacobs's dream at Bethel (Genesis 28:10–22)

Jacob's wrestling with the mysterious angel at Peniel
(Genesis 32:23–32)

Joseph's terrestrial and celestial dreams (Genesis 37:5–11)

The call of Isaiah (Isaiah 6:1–8)

The call of Jeremiah (Jeremiah 1:4–10)

The call of Ezekiel (Ezekiel 1:26—2:5)

I was brought up in the Reformed section of the Church and was grounded in what I have called 'prophetic religion'. In my own case I had already experienced, from childhood, a mystical sense of 'presence' in the natural world. I have sometimes humorously said that I was Catholic by nature and Reformed by training! Therefore, when the warnings against 'mystical religion' began to be sounded from my more Calvinistic friends (do not blame Calvin for some of his followers!), I had already sensed the mystical soil in which the great prophetic passages of the Old Testament were rooted—so it was too late! I remember one of the Old Testament lecturers in Zürich warning us against any kind of mystical religion that deviated from a concept of the absolute transcendence of God. And I was amazed when he included in his warning some of the hymns of Charles Wesley, specifically mentioning 'Jesus, Lover of my Soul'!

I examined my own faith in the light of these warnings, and found that my appreciation of the prophetic elements of the Old and New Testaments were not only as deep as that of my fellow-students, but that some of them had nurtured a dogmatic mind-set in which the mystical elements of the Bible itself were suspect. At the same time I was reading some of the Catholic mystics—it was some years before I began to appreciate the mystical theology of the Orthodox Church.

So alongside some of the great evangelical and puritan divines I was imbibing Brother Lawrence, John of the Cross, together with the Carmelite, Benedictine and Franciscan traditions.

Cross-fertilization was also taking place, and I remember the immense delight I experienced in reading the book by the great Methodist, W.E. Sangster, called *The Pure in Heart*, in which he expounded the holiness teaching of some of the great Catholic mystics. Also, one of my Baptist colleagues, Terry, and myself began to meet weekly to pray and read A.W. Tozer and Andrew Murray—both of whom pointed us to the mystical tradition of prayer and holiness. Much of this was found in the medieval Church and the early Fathers. I'm happy to record that Terry is still a Baptist minister and comes to my hermitage twice a year for a 'theological day' which begins with the eucharist, and leads on to sharing in study, prayer and fellowship, which is sheer joy to us both—and ecumenically particularly fruitful.

It has been a long journey since those days, and I appreciate the biblical elements I experienced, though I've had to unlearn a lot, and throw overboard some of the fundamentalist baggage! I am no longer able to categorize my theological stance, though I'm happy to settle for Catholic/evangelical, with an openness to intellectual freedom, and an increasing participation in global spirituality, which is widening my horizons to take in the whole of our world and the whole created order.

I think of myself as an ecumenical Christian, and at this point I should acknowledge my debt to the person and work of Thomas Merton. In him I found a man who not only allowed the Spirit to free him from his early rigid dogmatism, but who actually undertook a pilgrimage which involved body, mind and spirit. He recorded each step along the way, and carried me with him a few years later. His pilgrimage is encapsulated by these memorable words which make my point:

This journey without maps leads him into rugged mountainous country where there are often mists and storms and where he is more and more alone. Yet at the same time, ascending the slopes in darkness, feeling more and more keenly his own emptiness, and with the winter wind blowing through his now tattered garments, he meets at times other travellers on the way, poor pilgrims as he is, and as solitary as he, belonging perhaps to other lands and other traditions. There are, of course, great differences between them, and yet they have much in common. Indeed, the Western contemplative can say that he feels himself much closer to the Zen monks of ancient Japan than to the busy and impatient men of the West, of his own country, who think in terms of money, power, publicity, machines, business, political advantage, military strategy—who seek, in a word, the triumphant affirmation of their own will, their own power, considered as the end for which they exist. Is not this perhaps the most foolish of all dreams, the most tenacious and damaging of illusions?[1]

Prophetic religion

In affirming the prophetic dimensions of the faith, I want to point up some of the emphases which I believe are important to maintain from the prophetic tradition.

The word 'prophet' comes from the Greek *prophetes*, meaning literally, 'one who speaks for or on behalf of God'. I am fond of saying that:

a priest stands before God for the people;

a prophet stands before the people for God.

Therefore, the prophetic word is by inspiration, and contains revelation. We have seen that the word 'inspiration' has to do with the breath of God, and in the Nicene Creed we confess the Holy Spirit 'who spoke by the prophets'. As distinct from the leaders of pagan cults, the biblical prophet does not practise magic. He cannot manipulate God, but on the contrary is under the divine constraint. The divine impulsion is spelled out in Jeremiah's cry:

O Lord, you have enticed me, and I was enticed;
you have overpowered me, and you have prevailed…
If I say, 'I will not mention him, or speak any more in his name,'
then within me there is something like a burning fire
shut up in my bones;
I am weary with holding it in, and I cannot. (Jeremiah 20:7, 9)

God said to Moses, 'I will raise up for them a prophet like you from among their own people; I will put my words in the mouth of the prophet, who shall speak to them everything I command' (Deuteronomy 18:18). As well as Moses, Samuel, Elijah and Elisha, there were four great writing prophets of the Old Testament (Isaiah, Jeremiah, Ezekiel and Daniel), and twelve minor prophets, as well as others who shared the prophetic role.

After four centuries of prophetic silence, John the Baptist appears as the last of the old prophets and the forerunner of Jesus. The whole prophetic tradition led up to Jesus, who was prophet, priest and king, and not simply the bearer of revelation, but himself the revelation of the Father's heart (John 14:8–14).

In the early Church the prophetic ministry is exercised by both men and women, including Agabus (Acts 21:10), Jude and Silas (Acts 15:32), and the four daughters of Philip (Acts 21:8–10). A wonderful woman who lived a life of prophecy and prayer between the Testaments is Anna, who has special mention with Simeon in Luke 2:36–38.

The transcendence of God is clearly marked in the prophetic action, for God is the wholly Other, the God of righteousness, who calls the sinful nation to repentance and amendment of life. When the people of Israel fall into sinful and idolatrous practices, giving themselves to the worship of immoral fertility gods and goddesses, suddenly the great prophet Elijah breaks in upon the scene, and the prophetic word of judgment is proclaimed:

> *Now Elijah the Tishbite, of Tishbe in Gilead, said to Ahab, 'As the Lord the God of Israel lives, before whom I stand, there shall be neither dew nor rain these years, except by my word.'*
>
> *(1 Kings 17:1)*

This is the power of the prophet. He represents the one true and only God, demands repentance and conversion, and causes profound fear and trembling with his word of judgment. He speaks a word of revelation because he is an instrument of the Spirit, and the breath of God speaks through him. His is not a sweet and comfortable word conjured up by human intelligence or reason, but a divine command from the mouth of God:

> *For my thoughts are not your thoughts,*
> *nor are your ways my ways, says the Lord.*
> *For as the heavens are higher than the earth,*
> *so are my ways higher than your ways*
> *and my thoughts than your thoughts. (Isaiah 55:8–9)*

The false dichotomy which arose between prophetic and mystical religion was based both on fear and misunderstanding. The fear is that somehow mystical religion blurs the uniqueness of God. Its closeness to nature is disturbing to some because it sounds too much like the celebration of fertility and nature in the old

Canaanite religion so opposed in the Old Testament. Together with this is the feeling that with such a religion morality is blunted, and that moral responsibility and individuality is in danger of being lost.

Mystical religion has always been aware of the importance of God in the natural order, and the call of God is primarily one of love, leading to union. The language used by the two traditions has a different emphasis, and whereas union with God is the goal of the mystical life, conformity of the human will to the divine will is paramount in the prophetic faith. There are differences of emphases, even paradoxes in the tension between transcendence and immanence, but if properly understood, prophetic religion is rooted in mystical soil. Confrontation with God in the experience of the prophet is shot through with mystical intuition and immediacy of experience of the divine.

As I have listened to the fears of the Reformed side I have found that they defined the meaning of mysticism too narrowly, and related it so closely with pagan mysticism that few Christian mystics would have recognized it. At the same time they broadened the understanding of the prophetic religion so widely that most mystics would feel at home in it.

The Christian faith holds neither the exclusivity of the stark monotheism of Islam, nor the popular polytheism of Hinduism.[2] The revelation of God in the Old Testament is not static, but of dynamic love and mercy. The fulness of the new covenant breaks upon us in the incarnation of God in Christ. The life, death and resurrection of Jesus leads to Pentecost, where not only is the threefold nature of God's person made clear, but the Spirit of God comes to indwell the Church and the individual believer. Thus the Church becomes the body of Christ, and the believer becomes the temple of the Holy Spirit (Ephesians 2:21, 22; 1 Corinthians 3:16).

Mystical religion

Mystical religion need deny nothing of the prophetic element of the Christian faith, but it is necessary to affirm that the religion of revelation already has a context. It is rooted into something older and more primitive in the best sense. Christian mystical theology presupposes continuity between God and his creation. Christians are not deists who believe in a faraway, absent creator who set the mechanistic process of the world going and then retired.

Mystics are not *pantheists*, but they are *panentheists*. The difference is that *pantheism* means literally that 'everything is God'—God is identified with the world and the transcendent element is altogether lost. *Pantheism* means that God equals nature! *Panentheism* means that everything is in God—in him we live, and move and have our being. He includes and penetrates the universe, but is infinitely more than it. God is behind, below and within the natural order, and is not circumscribed by it.

In affirming continuity between God and humankind, the mystical tradition affirms that the image of God in humanity is not completely obliterated or destroyed. It is distorted, broken and atrophied because human nature has fallen from the divine love and marred his image, but it may be repaired.

There is a human capacity and potential for a complete restoration of the image and likeness of God by the reconciling grace of Christ; the mystical journey is a pilgrimage from the land of unlikeness to restoration of the image, and union with God in love. The way lies through the fiery purgation of God's fire, until we are aflame with his love—and both of these are imaged in mystical and prophetic religion.

LET ME GUARD

the

HOLY FIRE

Jesus, confirm my heart's desire
To work, and speak, and think for Thee;
Still let me guard the holy fire,
And still stir up Thy gift in me.

GUARDING THE FIRE

The nature of the divine fire is that it cannot be extinguished. That is why Wesley calls it an 'inextinguishable blaze'. Even if the altar fire in the individual human heart dies by neglect or sin, yet the source of the flame continues to burn elsewhere. God's love is inextinguishable, and will burn until every lesser flame is drawn to the divine centre of the blaze. So take warning! The celestial fire is inextinguishable, but its terrestrial manifestation may suffer neglect, burn low and smoulder. That is why Wesley prays: 'Still let me guard the holy fire…'

Before I returned from my cold caravan to my present hermitage in 1993, I thought of converting a neighbouring barn into a hermit cell with a small pot-bellied stove, as there was an abundance of wood lying around. This would have been a constant reminder to me to guard the fire. Commissioner Brengle of the Salvation Army once gave this advice about tending such a stove:

keep the draught open;

clean the ashes out;

keep feeding the fuel.

From him the 'draught' would have been the wind of the Spirit, the ashes would have been the neglect of fervour, and the culmination of unconfessed and unforgiven sin, and the fuel would have been the word of God with constant prayer and watchfulness (Ephesians 6:18). This is plain, practical holiness teaching, for unless the altar of the heart is clean and constantly fed with fuel, the fire will not burn.

But there is another sense in which we should guard the fire, and this has to do with the mystical life, which is intimate and personal, and about which there is a certain interior constraint, so that it should not be gossiped about, but tended in the great secret place of prayer and love.

There are certain things which Jesus was reticent about. He told some who were healed not to spread it abroad (Mark 1:43–44), and he strictly charged his disciples not to speak of his coming

sufferings or the wonder of the transfiguration until after his resurrection (Mark 9:9, 30–31).

In the experience of Francis, during the early days of the
Franciscan Order, there was a reticence about speaking of the stig-
mata (Francis' Calvary wounds in hands, feet and side) because of
the sacred nature of that experience.

Therefore, although we are to spread abroad the good news of
the gospel, telling the world of God's loving invitation in the work
of evangelism, there are areas of the deeper life of prayer about
which we should be reticent. These can only be held in secret love
between the lover and the beloved, and sometimes shared with
your soul friend or the small group of intimate friends who understand the mystical way. They are part of the great 'open secret',
but a secret nevertheless. Jacopone da Todi, that most open of
mystical saints, spells it out in his poem 'Love that is Silent':[1]

> *Love, silent as the night*
> *Who not one word will say*
> *To those who have not sight!*
>
> *O Love, you lie concealed*
> *Through heat and storm and cold*
> *So none may guess or read*
> *Your secrets manifold;*
> *Lest thieves should soon grow bold*
> *To steal away your treasure,*
> *Snatch it and take to flight!*
>
> *Hidden, your secret fires*
> *More ardently shall glow;*
> *And he who holds you close*
> *Your fiercest heat shall know.*
> *But he who shouts abroad*
> *Your mysteries, will be wounded,*
> *Scorched by your fiery might.*
>
> *The man who strives to tell*
> *His secret joy within,*
> *In babbling he breaks forth;*

> *Before his words begin*
> *The bitter winds of sin*
> *Will storm and whirl around him*
> *And wreck his treasure bright.*

> *Let Silence, at your door*
> *Hold captive all your sighs;*
> *For Love has set them there,*
> *And will not let him rise;*
> *So shall you hold your prize*
> *That it may live within you,*
> *Not scattered left and right.*

> *For if your sighs come forth*
> *Then follows on your mind*
> *To wander far from home*
> *Leaving true love behind;*
> *So shall you never find*
> *That inward, perfect love,*
> *That treasure Infinite.*

What does this poem mean? Well in the first place, if some third party, even a friend, enquired into the personal, intimate and sexual life of a married friend or couple, they would be told to mind their own business! The reasons need not be spelled out. There is a certain interior constraint, not to say shyness, in speaking outside the intimate embrace of love which would cheapen and devalue the essence of the relationship—let alone the beloved one!

All the genuine mystics, though they cannot help the overflow of mystical love and the fervour of speaking of it, yet come to that place of ineffability, of bankruptcy of language and of spiritual reticence in opening up the intimate heart of the matter from their personal experience. When I have written close to the profound experiences of my soul,[2] I have had requests from people to 'go on from there', and to share with them in terms of mystical theology and of my own secret mountain paths which are hidden from human sight, both in mists and glory.[3] But this I cannot do, and for the reasons stated above. In any case, I don't always know which part of the mountain my feet are planted upon, and to have glimpsed the unitive life, which is the experience of complete union with God in Christ, is not to have attained it. I am reminded that John Bunyan said that there is a door to hell from the very gate of heaven.

Jacopone says that if such secrets are indiscriminately scattered, then thieves will steal away the treasure. Such babbling dissipates the glory, and the resulting storms will only blind the eyes and the mind of the babbler.

He goes on to say that if the secret and ardent fire of love remains hidden with the beloved, then the beloved will draw the lover closer and increase the fierce heat. The resulting silence will itself hold the lover captive; the beloved will dwell in the secret place and unite the lover to himself in fiery joy.

I shall go on, in a moment, to illustrate this a little further, but at this point it is appropriate to say that guarding the fire in this way actually stirs up a deeper longing for God in those who read prayerfully and who come to share with me in simple gospel openness.

There are times when a brother or sister in Christ comes with or without their agenda of hopes and fears, and we are led together into dimensions of silence, talking and direction that are simply 'given', and often do not follow the preparations I have made for them. We are caught up into glory, and it is not under our control, and does not necessarily answer our questions, but stirs up interior longing, tears or joy that we had not bargained for, or expected. This is simply because the fire has been guarded, and the flame has therefore not been blown about or snuffed out by the winds of inordinate curiosity, which can only lead to spiritual pride in the soul friend or penitent.

By that, I mean that so-called gurus or self-styled mystics may be proud of their teaching and communication, and followers may take pride in their Ignatian awareness, their Benedictine stability or their Franciscan spontaneity! That leads to a fall—as do all hypocrisies. There is no doubt about the simple genuineness revealed in this glimpse of Gandhi:

> Sometimes, if he was too tired, or the crowd too noisy, he would sit on the platform in silence until the crowd, which often numbered 200,000, became quiet. He then continued to sit in silence, and

*the men and women sat in silence, and he touched his palms
together to please them, and smiled and departed. This was communication without words, and the mass silence was an exercise in
self-control and self-searching, a step therefore towards self-rule.*[4]

Living flame of love

Having said all that, and still guarding the interior fire, I want to
share as much of the great mystical tradition as I can, illustrating
from my own limited experience, while heeding the precedent set
by John of the Cross. After expounding his poem 'Living Flame of
Love', he stops short of describing mystical union with God in
prose, first because he realizes that he is incapable of communicating its reality and, second, because if he were to try, he would
fall utterly short of its glory.[5]

But what he cannot spell out in prose he certainly communicates in the language of the soul of his poetry. I remember, in my
twenties, being stricken by the stanza which has captivated my
heart ever since:

> *How gently and how lovingly*
> *You lie awake in my bosom*
> *Where alone You secretly dwell;*
> *And in Your sweet breathing,*
> *Full of grace and glory,*
> *How tenderly You fill me*
> *With Your love.*

Ever since then, I have read and learned his poetry, puzzled over
his commentaries, and sought, through scripture and the mystical
tradition, a deeper understanding and a profounder experience of
the mystery of God.

I have found and continue searching, as I have been found by
the God who continues to search and yearn for me. And though
there are times of immense joy and tears, there are also times
when I realize that I have hardly begun. Let me set out a beautiful
new translation of 'The Living Flame of Love' in a new book on
John of the Cross:

Flame, alive, compelling,
yet tender past all telling,
reaching the secret centre of my soul!
Since now evasions over,
finish your work, my Lover,
break the last thread, wound me and make me whole!

Burn that is for my healing!
Wound of delight past feeling!
Ah, gentle hand whose touch is a caress,
foretaste of heaven conveying
and every debt repaying:
slaying, you give me life for death's distress.

O lamps of fire bright-burning
with splendid brilliance, turning
deep caverns of my soul to pools of light!
Once shadowed, dim, unknowing,
now their strange new-found glowing
gives warmth and radiance for my Love's delight.

Ah, gentle and so loving
you wake within me, proving
that you are there in secret and alone;
your fragrant breathing stills me,
your grace, your glory fills me
so tenderly your love becomes my own.[6]

Some of author Iain Matthew's comments on this poem only emphasize what I have been saying. In the context of the words 'the more infectious his wonder, the less informative it is', he goes on:

The verbs are about what 'you' are doing. You are piercing, repaying, slaying, giving life, waking, breathing; you did seem oppressive, but it was you that seemed it; you may tear the veil, but it has to be you. If 'my' soul gives radiance it is because you shine on it; and if 'I' love it is because your love awakens me.

When John comments on his verses, the pervasive feature is the same. His God anticipates, initiates, gives, transforms; like a flame entering till it engages the 'deepest centre'. John's universe is drenched in a self-outpouring God.

The commentary presents a strange world; to survive it, we must suspend disbelief. Its pages breathe rhapsody. They are peppered with exclamations—'Oh...! How...!'—which, the author maintains, mean what they say: 'affection and praise'. In The Living Flame, John comes wide-eyed, not to explain, but to say thank you.[7]

Stricken by love

Decades have now passed since my first encounter with the poetry of John of the Cross. The first lessons I had to learn, after the Lord had taken me prisoner by the erotic power of the poetry, was that the path of mystical prayer was not an erotic or carnal path, though the Spirit of God does possess the believer in body, soul and spirit. After the wonder of evangelical conversion and an intoxicating introduction to the mystical path, I had to travel a long path of penitence and asceticism, without losing the spontaneity and joy of the gospel.

As these two things went hand in hand, asceticism and mysticism, discipline and spontaneity, tears and ecstasy, I began to understand that the penitence and asceticism of John was in order that the believer might more surely pursue the way of the divine love—or rather that the believer might be made receptive and open to the invasion of the divine lover. I remember the day when I came across the stanza:

> *If then, on the common land,*
> *From henceforth I am neither seen nor found,*
> *You will say that I am lost;*
> *That wandering love-stricken,*
> *I lost my way and was found.*

It was with sheer delight and relief that I saw myself pictured in the commentary:

In this stanza the soul answers a tacit reproof of those in the world who usually criticize persons who are entirely given to God and think these persons excessive in their conduct, estrangement and withdrawal, and assert that they are useless in important matters and lost to what the world esteems. The soul skilfully answers this reprimand, boldly facing it and all the other possible reproofs of the world; for in having reached the intimate love of God, she considers everything else of little consequence.[8]

Guarding & sharing

Back in early days of my Christian journey, a group of us used to cover the pubs in the seedier part of Swansea on a Saturday night. We had scores of conversations (and confrontations!) each week, which often turned out to be real evangelistic opportunities. Such evangelism might be frowned upon by the respectable church-going establishment, but they were in direct line with both the Franciscan and Wesleyan practices of their day.

I was full of fervour and joy on these occasions, but well I remember one evening in the darkness, leaning against the wall opposite the Rum 'n' Punch pub, completely inebriated (not with alcohol because I was a teetotaller) with the joy and love of God. I could hardly stand up, and after a while one of the fellows found me. He had not seen me like this before, so it took a bit of understanding. The result of that was that I thought and prayed through it, and realized that I was not 'guarding the fire' but letting it obviously be seen, for what was affecting me was not simple exuberant pentecostal joy, but profound intoxication with the love of Christ. This is akin to the experience that the apostle Paul guarded with great care (2 Corinthians 12:2–4). My friend's comments called me back to order and discipline. Over the years I have become aware that although the situation described by John of the Cross may be a living, puzzling, wonderful reality in my spiritual journey, there must be a guarding of such intimate moments or periods, save when it is clearly God's will for them to be shared in an appropriate time and place.

This chapter is not meant to guard the fire in the sense of making it an esoteric, gnostic knowledge only for the élite or the elect. Neither does it deny that we must joyfully proclaim the saving gospel of Christ and the gifts of the Spirit. Indeed, the remaining chapters in this section share a great deal of mystical experience and charism. But always there is this sense of 'guarding' the fire from the merely curious and contemptuous gaze, and from a mere babbling of our mystical experience, for that will simply dissipate its heat.

So bearing in mind the loving secrecy between lover and beloved, we shall now go on to experiential and mystical teaching which shares the light and heat of the beloved—with proper reverence and regard for the mystery.

LIGHT & FIRE

Fill me, radiancy divine

One of the most precious experiences of my life took place during the hermit symposium which met for a week in the summer of 1976 at St David's, Wales. It was a unique gathering of about thirty (mostly) hermits, and there is a direct line from that week to my present exploration of the hermit life.

It was at one of those early morning eucharists, and I don't remember whether it was Orthodox, Roman Catholic or Anglican rite. What I do remember is that in the midst of the silence, incense and liturgy, the early sun broke through the clear windows of the chapel behind the cathedral high altar, and we began to sing Charles Wesley's hymn 'Christ Whose Glory Fills the Skies'. It was an experience of what the Russian Orthodox call *Sobornost*, the kind of fellowship engendered by the Holy Spirit, which causes the worshippers to tremble with joy and adoration:

> *Visit then this soul of mine;*
> *Pierce the gloom of sin and grief;*
> *Fill me, radiancy divine;*
> *Scatter all my unbelief;*
> *More and more thyself display,*
> *Shining to the perfect day.*[1]

The Wesley hymns are full of light and fire, and I have been struck recently, in reading the story of Symeon the New Theologian (AD949–1022),[2] how much one puts me in mind of the other.

The Discourses of Symeon are full of light and fire, and so many parallels can be drawn theologically and spiritually, even to the persecutions they underwent because of the evangelical and mystical emphases in the experience of God in conversion and holiness.

It is difficult to choose particular passages to demonstrate the reality of the divine light in the experience of Symeon, but there are three which show progression and maturity in his pilgrimage.

The first took place when he was twenty years of age, and he writes of himself in the third person:

> As he stood and recited, 'God, have mercy upon me, a sinner' *(Luke 18:13)*, uttering it with his mind rather than his mouth, suddenly a flood of divine radiance appeared from above and filled all the room. As this happened the young man lost all awareness *(of his surroundings)* and forgot that he was in a house or that he was under a roof. He saw nothing but light all around him and did not know if he was standing on the ground. He was not afraid of falling; he was not concerned with the world, nor did anything pertaining to men and corporeal beings enter his mind. Instead, he was wholly in the presence of immaterial light and seemed to himself to have turned into light. Oblivious of all the world, he was filled with tears and ineffable joy and gladness.[3]

The second experience of light took place when he was a novice. His spiritual father, Symeon the Studite, had wept with him because of the mercy and love of God, and told him to return to his cell and recite the Trisagion ('Holy God, Holy and Mighty, Holy and Immortal, have mercy upon us').

No sooner had he begun to repeat the words 'Holy God...' than he began to weep with loving desire for God. He fell prostrate on to the ground surrounded again, by what he calls 'immaterial light' shining upon and within him. Beginning to cry 'Lord, have mercy' he entered into an ecstasy and when he came to himself he found he was still reciting the words, and he describes it:

> 'Whether I was in the body, or outside the body' *(2 Corinthians 12:2–3)*, I conversed with this Light. The Light itself knows it; it scattered whatever mist there was in my soul and cast out every earthly care. It expelled from me all material denseness and bodily heaviness that made my members to be sluggish and numb. What an awesome marvel! It so invigorated and strengthened my limbs and muscles, which had been faint with weariness, that it seemed to me as though I was stripping myself of the garment of corruption. Besides, there was poured into my soul in unutterable fashion a great spiritual joy, and perception and a sweetness

surpassing every taste of visible objects, together with a freedom of forgetfulness of all thoughts pertaining to this life. In a marvellous way there was granted to me and revealed to me the manner of the departure from this present life. Thus all the perceptions of my mind and my soul were wholly concentrated on the ineffable joy of that Light.[4]

This second visitation penetrated deeper, and the similarities between Wesley's prayer above, and the experience of Symeon are clear. It was an experience which scattered Symeon's unbelief, expelled sluggishness of mind and body, invigorated physical life, imparted joy and spiritual awareness and gave foretaste of the life to come. Yet it was transient, for he immediately goes on to say that it gently and calmly faded, causing great loneliness and sadness. His heart burned with the pain of separation, and he longed for the return of such infinite love.

The third experience is described in Symeon's last disclosure, and transformed his life permanently. If the first experience of light took place in his immature days of early conversion, and the second experience penetrated deeper in the work of sanctification, then the third exposure to the divine light was a breakthrough.

His final discourse is in the form of a testimony and thanksgiving for the ecstatic and mystical visitation of God throughout his life, and during the twenty or so years as abbot, exile and spiritual director. His biographer, Nicetas, says that the power of the Spirit 'was stirring and leaping within him, not allowing him any repose until he had put into writing His words and interior operations'.

So, after recording an account of 'the terrifying and attractive beauty of God' throughout his life, he speaks of a period of silence and waiting, with an interior mingling of unutterable joy and weeping sorrow in yearning to be completely united with God in light and love.

He describes himself standing before the icon of the *Theotokos* (Mary the God-bearer), and he goes on:

As I fell before it, before I rose up, Thou Thyself didst appear to me within my poor heart, as though Thou hadst transformed it into light; and then I knew that I have Thee consciously within me. From then onwards I loved Thee, not by recollection of Thee and

97

that which surrounds Thee, nor for the memory of such things, but
I in very truth believed that I had Thee, substantial love, within
me. For Thou, O God, truly art love. (1 John 4:8, 16)[5]

From this time on, the light never leaves him, day or night, eating
or drinking, waking or sleeping. He is united with the light which
is the love of God in Christ, by the interior transformation of the
Holy Spirit.

In his chapter 'The Divine Light' Vladimir Lossky speaks of the
uncreated light in which God reveals and communicates himself
to those who enter into union with him. He says that the mystical
light of the transfiguration, which is reflected in Symeon, Gregory
Palamas, Seraphim, and other such saints, is not merely the symbol of intellectual understanding. Nor is it just a visible and sen-
sual light, though it may flood the whole being, including the
mind and heart. It is the uncreated light of God which shines forth
from his essence and is revealed in his energies. This is the light of
transfiguration, radiating from the Holy Spirit:

The sight of the eye and the sight of the mind do not perceive one
and the same light, but it is the property of each of these faculties
to act according to its own nature and limitations. Since, however,
those who are worthy of it receive spiritual and supernatural grace
and strength, they perceive, both by the sense and by the intellect
that which is altogether above both sense and intellect... but this
light is known only to God and to those who have had experience
of his grace.[6]

The New Testament is full of the light and glory of spiritual experience, and Paul writes a marvellous chapter about the Holy Spirit
as the outshining radiance of God in the second letter to the
Corinthians. After speaking of the fading light and glory of the
holy covenant reflected on the face of Moses, he says that the
Spirit of God shines with gospel light upon us, and we reflect back
that glory, while we are being transformed from one degree of
glory to another (2 Corinthians 3:18). Then he links the Spirit's
light which shone in the darkness and chaos at creation with the
gospel light which illumines the heart of the believer:

For it is the God who said, 'Let light shine out of darkness,' who has shone in our hearts to give the light of the knowledge of the glory of God in the face of Jesus Christ. (2 Corinthians 4:6)

Light & fire

Seraphim of Sarov, the saintly Russian mystic of eighteenth-century Russia, begins his spiritual teaching with these perceptive words:

God is a fire which warms and kindles our hearts. If we feel in our hearts the cold which comes from the devil—for the devil is cold—let us pray to the Lord, and he will come and warm our hearts with love for him and love for our neighbour. And before the warmth of his face, the cold of the enemy will be put to flight.[7]

This is the warm heart experienced by the Emmaus walkers as the risen Christ dispelled the icy coldness of doubt and grief (Luke 24:32), and which warmed the heart of John Wesley as the scriptures were expounded in that Moravian meeting in 1738.

Fire is a complex symbol, for it may signify the divine presence, the divine love, the transcendence and holiness of God, and his purifying power. What is the purifying nature of God's flaming love on the one hand is the destruction of evil by that same love on the other. It is the same sun which melts the wax and hardens the clay!

We may trace the fiery sign of God's presence and revelation throughout the Old Testament:

to Abraham in the flaming torch (Genesis 15:17–18)

to Moses at the burning bush (Exodus 3:2–3)

to Moses on the summit of Sinai (Exodus 19:18–19)

to Elijah on Mount Carmel (1 Kings 18:38)

to Elijah in the fiery chariot (2 Kings 2:11)

to Elisha in the flaming mountain chariots (2 Kings 6:17)

in the perpetual altar of fire (Leviticus 6:12–13)

in the guiding pillar of fire for Israel (Exodus 13:21)

in the prophetic call of Isaiah (Isaiah 6:6–8)

in the prophetic call of Ezekiel (Ezekiel 1:27)

And we may add to that list of the old covenant prophets the first of the new, John the Baptist, who proclaimed that Jesus 'will baptize you with the Holy Spirit and fire' (Luke 3:16).

Macarius of Egypt, the fourth-century desert monk, says that the fire of grace kindled in the hearts of Christians by the Holy Spirit makes them burn like candles before the Son of God, and he evokes the New Testament images of fire:

> *The immaterial and divine fire enlightens and tests souls. This fire descended upon the apostles in the form of fiery tongues; this fire shone upon Paul, it spoke to him, it enlightened his mind, and at the same time it blinded his eyes, for flesh cannot bear the brightness of this light.*[8]

Apart from the 'Living Flame of Love' poem and commentary of John of the Cross, he also uses fire as an analogy of the burning holiness of God in the image of the log, which is the human experience of sanctification.

The process is that a damp log is being taken up into the warmth, light and heat of the fire. The divine light, which acts upon the soul in purging and preparing it for perfect union with God, acts as fire upon the log of wood, in order to transform it into itself.

First, the fire begins to dry it, driving out and expelling the moisture. This makes it black and unsightly, and as it dries gradually it gives out a bad smell. But the process drives out all the unsightly accidents which are contrary to the nature of fire. As it continues, the purging gives way to kindling, to warmth and heat, and finally there is the transformation into the beauty and wonder of its own nature. The log becomes the fire, and the fire burns fiercely.[9]

Fiery judgment

These chapters speak of the graciousness of God in illuminating us with his light, and warming us with his fire, and it would seem that anyone would desire such illumination and warmth. But it is clear from the mystics of East and West that the mystical path is one which is not to be taken lightly. They would all agree that the way to union in love involves much suffering.

Light can be an agonizing experience for sore eyes, and fire is dangerous and life-threatening when out of control. Neither of these are in our power or subject to our will. I have pointed out that there is a certain passivity and receptivity required of us. Only as we yield ourselves in this way shall we feel the call to the mystical path, and only when that comes will we be able to choose.

There is at work a kind of synergism, a 'working together' of the Spirit's call and the human response. The path begins with penitence, and this teaches the soul a certain humility before God, with an increasing reverence and awe at the approach of the divine light and fire. We have understood this, in part, when we spoke of 'guarding the fire'.

But now let us turn to a profound insight of Orthodoxy which differentiates between the essence and energies of God. This will enable us the better to understand how a human being can begin to know, and then to experience and love, the God who is incomprehensible to the human mind as it wanders in the region of unlikeness to God.

THE ENERGIES OF LOVE

Essence & energies

There are a number of paradoxes in the Bible which we must hold together in creative tension, truths which pressed to an extreme would become contradictory or heretical. Among them are the transcendence (otherness) and the immanence (nearness) of God, divine sovereignty and human responsibility, faith and works, grace and nature.

The paradox presented in this chapter is the Bible's witness of God as incomprehensible, unknowable in his inner essence, and the revelation and experience of God in his acts of power and healing love, called his energies. The first is illustrated by 1 Timothy 6:15–16:

> …the blessed and only Sovereign, the King of kings and Lord of lords. It is he alone who has immortality and dwells in unapproachable light, whom no one has ever seen or can see; to him be honour and eternal dominion. Amen.

The second is illustrated by 2 Peter 1:4:

> Thus he has given us, through these things, his precious and very great promises, so that through them you may escape from the corruption that is in the world… and may become participants of the divine nature.

The first text tells us that God, in his essence, is inaccessible, and the second that God, by his grace and energies, is accessible. Both these poles of essence and energies are reflected in John 1:18: 'No one has ever seen God. It is God the only Son, who is close to the Father's heart, who has made him known.'

The Eastern Fathers made such statements as: 'He is outside all things according to his essence, but he is in all things through his acts of power' (Athanasius). And: 'No one has ever seen the essence of God, but we believe in the essence because we experience the energy' (Basil).

When we speak of God's essence we mean his utter transcendence, his otherness, and by his energies we mean his immanence, his nearness. We can never know God in his innermost essence (neither can the angels or archangels!), for if we could, we would be God, knowing him in the same way that he knows himself. But we can truly know God by his energies, grace, life and power which are manifested through the whole universe and are directly accessible to us. God is God, and we are his creatures, and though he may wholly possess us, we may not wholly possess him.

If we make this distinction between the essence and energies of God, we are able to understand that we may truly participate in the life and nature of God by grace, just as we are able to participate in the healing rays of the sun, though not penetrate the sun's essence. As Gregory Palamas put it:

> As the sun, according to the divine dispensation, tempering the vigour and sincerity of its rays by the intermediate air, emits to those receiving it a proportionate splendour and heat, remaining by itself unapproachable to the weakness of our nature, thus also the divine power, by a similarity to the given example, infinitely surpassing our nature and inaccessible to participation… gives to the human nature what is in her power to receive.[1]

Mystical union is real union with God by virtue of his energies—what the Greek Fathers called *theosis*, which may be translated divinization, or deification. Such a distinction makes us real participants without losing our identity in some kind of pantheism, for we participate in the energies, and not the essence. We are 'oned' with God, but not annihilated!

In an excellent chapter on God's uncreated energies of love, George Maloney states the distinction succinctly:

> Eastern Christian theologians developed the distinction between the divine essence and God's uncreated energies. This distinction is a means of explaining how God's being is unknowable to us in his essence, and yet God does truly communicate himself to us in a new knowledge and a new participation through his uncreated energies. The energies are God's mode of existing in relationship

to his created world, especially to us. Such a distinction is not often made use of in Western Christianity, where God also is believed to be absolute and essentially unknowable in his divine nature. Nevertheless, he does relate himself to the created order and so is knowable to us through his created energies of love.[2]

Language of paradox & symbolism

The only language we have is human language, and we have to pull and stretch it, and resort to analogies, pictures and symbols when we speak of the divine. For instance, when we speak of God as dwelling in light or darkness (and scripture does both), these are signs of symbols used by the scripture and mystical writers as parables or analogies of God in his relation with us.[3]

God is sometimes referred to as 'dazzling darkness' or 'luminous darkness', and such language is for our sakes—the darkness is in us and not in him. Dionysius the Areopagite, the sixth-century Syrian monk, says that the divine darkness is the inaccessible light in which God dwells, but we must remember that to God darkness and light are both alike (Psalm 139:12). Such paradoxical language is affirming that God is the fulness of glory and love beyond our understanding, and it is well to remember the German theologian Jacob Boehme's words: 'The darkness is not the absence of light, but the terror that comes from the blinding light.' The paradox is stated by William Johnston in this way:

We know God; and we do not know God. God is the mystery of mysteries; we know that he is, but we do not know what he is. No one has seen God who dwells in inaccessible light which is impenetrable darkness. And yet we do know God. We can become very intimate with God who spoke to Moses as one might speak to a friend. Friendship with God is the great privilege and joy of the one who believes; it is the consolation of the mystic.[4]

The doctrine of the energies is the key to real mystical experience of God. For God, who is inaccessible in his essence, is available in his energies; incomprehensible in his essence, yet revealed in his energies. As Johnston says again:

These uncreated energies, then, are nothing other than the Triune God in his dynamic and loving action. God who is love dwells within and generates a tremendous energy (or, more correctly, God is a tremendous energy) which overflows on the senses, paradoxically causing intense delight and suffering. This fits the experience of many mystics.[5]

Life within the Holy Spirit

The word *theosis* means that we truly participate in the trinitarian life of God, but we do not *become* the trinity, for we participate by grace. Vladimir Lossky, the Orthodox theologian, expounds the doctrine of the uncreated energies of God within their trinitarian context. He quotes Gregory of Thessalonica:

Just as God is at the same time both one and three, 'the divine nature must be said to be at the same time both exclusive of, and, in some sense, open to participation. We attain to participation in the divine nature, and yet at the same time it remains totally inaccessible. We need to affirm both at the same time and to preserve the antimony as a criterion of right devotion.[6]

Lossky sets mystical experience in the light of the Trinity when he says:

The divine promise cannot be an illusion; we are called to participate in the divine nature. We are therefore compelled to recognize in God an ineffable distinction, other than that between His essence and His persons, according to which He is, under different aspects, both totally inaccessible and at the same time accessible. This distinction is that between the essence of God, or His nature, properly so-called, which is inaccessible, unknowable and incommunicable; and the energies or divine operations, forces proper to and inseparable from God's essence, in which He goes forth from Him Himself, manifests, communicates, and gives Himself.[7]

In one sense, the whole of the Bible as the revelation of God is the story of the abounding revelatory energies of God, manifesting his glory in the world. The 'glory' is the outshining of his grace, and therefore we read of:

> the 'Father of Glory' (Ephesians 1:17), who manifests wisdom, revelation, knowledge, power and holiness;

> the Son, 'the reflection of God's glory (Hebrews 1:3), who is 'the exact imprint of God's very being', who accomplishes the work of redemption and reconciliation;

> the 'spirit of glory' (1 Peter 4:14), who fills believers with joy in the suffering and exalted Christ, even in the midst of persecution and trials.

There is a unique interior glory of God's trinitarian life and essence which is incommunicable and incomprehensible, but there is the glory of the Father, Son and Spirit which is poured forth in the uncreated energies of love and grace, in which he manifests, communicates, reveals and unfolds his blessedness in sharing it with those he has created and redeemed in love. Both the inner trinitarian mystery and the joyful rapture of the redeemed is reflected in this verse by Charles Wesley:

> *While the army above*
> *Overwhelmed by his love,*
> *The Trinity sings*
> *With their faces enwrapp'd in the shadowing wings,*
> *Holy Father, we cry,*
> *Holy Son, we reply,*
> *Holy Spirit of grace,*
> *And extol the Three-One in a rapture of praise.*[8]

When redeemed humankind truly participates in this glory, the image and likeness of God is restored and, as in a mirror, the divine glory is reflected back in a circular dance and game of love (2 Corinthians 3:18).

Holistic practice

If this is your first introduction to the Eastern distinction between the essence and energies of God, it will take some prayerful reflection to realize how important the distinction is. It not only has doctrinal importance in understanding better the wonder of God's mystery, but it has practical implications. The overflowing energies of grace is the experience of love, and such energies are directed not only to the renewal of the human spirit in the likeness of God's image, but to the illumination of the mind, and the participation of the body. I say 'participation' of the body, for the wholeness of our salvation in complete healing and resurrection will not be consummated until the *parousia*, the second advent of Christ in glory. But the experience of the energies of God's grace and love is an holistic unity, and the body is meant to participate (Romans 8:11). The promise and hope is made clear in Paul's prayer:

> *May the God of peace himself sanctify you entirely; and may your spirit and soul and body be kept sound and blameless at the coming of our Lord Jesus Christ. The one who calls you is faithful, and he will do this.* (1 Thessalonians 5:23–24)

An holistic approach means that although we distinguish between spirit, soul and body, we hold them together in the entirety of which Paul speaks. We have been used to believing that God works within our spirit, giving us new birth to what we used to call 'our soul's salvation', and also that our minds and intellects are renewed by the light from scripture and church teaching. But we are realizing more and more that salvation is for the whole person. When Jesus was confronted with human need, he applied his healing energies and his forgiving love to the whole man, woman or child, and salvation was an holistic compassion directed to the healing of the whole world.

The energies of God's love are at work, and now we shall turn to an ancient way of praying, using the body, rooted in the Greek *hesychast* tradition, and in which there is increasing practical interest.

THE PRAYER OF QUIET

Quiet, stillness, tranquillity

The *hesychast* was a monk who practised the desert spirituality of *hesychasm*. The word *hesychia* is the Greek word for quiet, stillness, tranquillity, and at its most profound is thought to be a foretaste of the experience of the saints in heaven, who no longer need liturgical or private prayers, but live wholly in God.

> *As the saints in the world to come no longer pray, their minds having been engulfed in the divine Spirit, but dwell in ecstasy in that excellent glory; so the mind, when it has been made worthy of perceiving the blessedness of the age to come, will forget itself and all that is here, and will no longer be moved by the thought of anything.*[1]

According to the seventh-century teacher Isaac the Syrian, this is the perfecting of prayer in contemplation when the mind has ascended above prayer, and having found what is more excellent, desists from prayer. Kallistos Ware is careful to point out that for most people this is not a permanent state:

> The *hesychast, as well as entering into the prayer of stillness, uses other forms of prayer as well, sharing corporate liturgical worship, reading scripture, receiving the sacraments.*[2]

The trouble with defining such terms as *hesychia* in such idealistic ways seems to put it out of the reach of most of us. The truth is that it is meant to lead us on gently but surely into the simple joy of walking and living in the Spirit, which is meant to be the norm for all Christians.

When John Wesley taught that beyond evangelical conversion there was a progressive path of sanctification which led to what he called 'perfection' or 'perfect love', he was not claiming an élitist kind of sinlessness. It was his way of affirming that we should strive for perfection, and not be content with what we are saved *from*.

From his early days, he studied patristics, and in his Address to the Clergy in 1756, he made it very clear:

Can any who spend several years in those seats of learning be excused if they do not add to that of the languages and sciences, the knowledge of the fathers—the most authentic commentators on scripture, as being both nearest the fountain and eminently endued with the Spirit by whom 'all scripture was given' [see 2 Timothy 3:16]... I speak chiefly of those who wrote before the Council of Nicaea. But who would not likewise desire to have some acquaintance with those that followed them—with Chrysostom, Basil, Jerome, Austin and, above all, the man of a broken heart, Ephraim Syrus?[3]

Albert Outler, the Methodist scholar, calls attention to the fact that John Wesley studied the Greek Fathers from the early Holy Club days, with men like his fellow-Methodist John Clayton, who was a competent patristic scholar. The influence of Gregory of Nyssa, through Macarius the Egyptian, led Wesley to an understanding of *teleiosis* or perfection, as the goal of true spirituality and prayer. As Outler says:

Thus in his early days he drank deep of this Byzantine tradition of spirituality at its source and assimilated its conception of devotion as the way, *and perfection as the* goal *of the Christian life.*[4]

Thus Wesley the evangelist sought to proclaim and spread the fire of God's consuming love for a lost world, and Wesley the teacher of perfection sought to tend and guard the holy fire of love for the beloved, which is interior, secret and kept from the carnal gaze of the curious. I should like to hear John Wesley's comment on this definition of *hesychasm*:

Hesychasm: This refers to the type of 'desert' spirituality that started in the fourth century with the development in the Egyptian and Mesopotamian deserts of various forms of monasticism. Men and women live a way of life made up of intense ascetical practices of solitude, the guarding of one's thoughts, and purification of the 'heart' by fasting, vigils, and incessant prayer which included synchronizing one's breathing with the name of Jesus. The goal was to attain transformation by the uncreated energies of God-Trinity into their divinized true selves as in their humanity they fulfilled God's eternal plan to make all of us in God's image and likeness.[5]

Hesychasm for all

Generally *hesychasm* is the way of inner prayer taught and practised in the Christian East from the fourth century, but this is not confined to the monk or hermit. Gregory of Nyssa says that Mary, the mother of Jesus, was introduced at the age of three into the Holy of Holies in the temple, to give herself up to *hesychia*, silent contemplation, though it isn't clear where he gets his information!

For us, *hesychia* is 'returning into ourselves', guarding the heart with watchfulness, not only from curious intruders, but also against evil thoughts and distractions. John Climacus says that the *hesychast* strives to confine his spiritual self within his bodily house. This leads to the kind of contemplative prayer that is free from discursive meditation, images and concepts, and leads to stillness in the Holy Spirit.

William Johnston's 'Main characteristics of *Hesychasm*' links us with our earlier context of prayer as Light and Fire:

1. Entering into a state of *quiet* without reading or thinking or reasoning or imagining.

2. Repeating the *Jesus Prayer*: 'Lord Jesus Christ, Son of God, have mercy on me, a sinner.' What matters is the name of Jesus, which, when recited with faith and love, has power to move heaven and earth.

3. Regulating the *breathing*, so that it becomes rhythmical. The aim is to allow the mind to descend into the heart.

4. Feeling the inner *warmth*, or experiencing the divine light, sometimes called 'the light of Tabor'.

5. The aim of all is deification or *theosis*.[6]

I have written elsewhere of the Jesus Prayer,[7] but it is worth noting that when the anonymous nineteenth-century Russian peasant[8] sought the meaning of praying without ceasing, he found help with an old monk-*staretz* who quoted Symeon the New Theologian:

> *Sit down alone and in silence. Lower your head, shut your eyes,*
> *breathe out gently and imagine yourself looking into your own*
> *heart. Carry your mind to your heart. As you breathe out say,*
> *'Lord Jesus Christ, have mercy on me.' Say it moving your lips*
> *gently or simply say it in your mind. Try to put all other thoughts*
> *aside. Be calm, be patient and repeat the process very frequently.*[9]

In the story told by the peasant we have the unfolding, from complete ignorance to the development of spiritual experience, with practical instruction from the *staretz* and the written tradition. This leads to the peasant's personal participation in the dynamic reality of real experience of God—which is the work of *theosis*. It is simple enough for anyone, yet profound beyond comprehension.

The pilgrim possesses a knapsack with some dried bread and a Bible, and as he tramps through Siberia, to the tomb of Innocent of Irkutsk, the Lord visits him with the gift of grace which is the Jesus Prayer:

> *After no great lapse of time I had the feeling that the Prayer had,*
> *so to speak, by its own action passed from my lips to my heart,*
> *that is to say, it seemed as though my heart in its ordinary beat-*
> *ing began to say the words of the Prayer within at each beat. Thus*
> *for example one, 'Lord', two, 'Jesus', three, 'Christ', and so on.*
> *I simply listened carefully to what my heart was saying. It seemed*
> *as though my eyes looked right down into it; and I dwelt upon the*
> *words of my departed* staretz *when he was telling me about this*
> *joy. Then I felt something like a slight pain in my heart, and in my*
> *thoughts so great a love for Jesus Christ that I pictured myself, if*
> *only I could see Him, throwing myself at His feet and not letting*
> *them go from my embrace, kissing them tenderly, and thanking*
> *Him with tears for having of His love and grace allowed me to find*
> *so great a consolation in His Name, me, His unworthy and sinful*
> *creature! Further there came into my heart a gracious warmth*
> *which spread through my whole breast.*[10]

This is one of the strands of *hesychasm*—a simple method of opening yourself to the presence of God, allowing your mind to descend to the heart, and repeating the Jesus Prayer. It can be done with the rhythm of the breathing or heartbeat, and it is simply repeated, sitting, kneeling or walking.

Continuing this practice in loving faith, eventually the prayer will take root in the heart, or, to use other analogies, a small fire will begin to burn, or a murmuring stream will spring up. This fulfils the promise of Jesus regarding the indwelling Spirit who will cause rivers of living water to flow from the believer's innermost being (John 7:37–39).

Psychosomatic unity

One of the lovely things about *hesychasm*, and the practice of the Jesus Prayer is that of the importance of the body, the heart and the breathing. We are incarnate beings, and it is important that salvation touches, redeems and sanctifies every part of us. *Theosis* or divinization is the work of the life-giving Spirit in raising the human spirit to the life of God, illuminating the mind, and giving healing to the physical body.

This does not mean that we are immediately made perfect in spirit, soul and body. The fulness of such a redeeming process will only come to fruition in the life of heaven. But it does mean that it begins now, and is immediately available, though not yet in its fulness.

If I approach the living presence of God through scripture, through sacrament and through prayer, I am brought into spiritual renewal; if I need clarity of mind in the things of God I ask for the Spirit's illumination; if I suffer sickness or infirmity, I seek through charismatic and sacramental healing the anointing and healing of the Spirit (James 5:13–16).

Thus heaven can begin today in my soul; eternal life is already rooted within me; I already have glimpses of the prayer of quiet, and the unitive life which is the life of heaven.

If such a holistic experience of salvation is manifest among the people of God, then the effects will be felt first of all within the community of faith. Then it will spread to the surrounding community of family, friends and neighbourhood, reaching out into the world of suffering, injustice and conflict.

This brings us to our last section, in which Wesley's hymn speaks of the perfect will of God being done within our present lives on earth, and in which dying is one of the mercies which leads us, at last, to the perfection of life in heaven.

ALL THY PERFECT WILL

Ready for all Thy perfect will,
My acts of faith and love repeat,
Till death Thy endless mercies seal,
And make the sacrifice complete.

CHRIST-CENTRED
MYSTICISM

As Charles Wesley brings his brief hymn to a close, he writes of our being made ready for the perfect will of God to become operative in our lives. Our acts of personal and corporate faith and love should manifest that will on earth, as it is in heaven. Only then can we confidently move towards the sealing of God's endless mercies in a good death, which will carry us through that last earthly barrier, to continue the pilgrimage in the eternal love in heaven. In this last section we shall endeavour to discern what God's perfect will for us means, ask how it may be lived out in our contemporary world, and then see how we may be able and willing to lay down our lives when the time comes, and enter glory.

Universal yet particular

One of the primary things we need to learn in our human and Christian lives is an attitude of openness to all. We are aware of the creative tension in affirming the universality of God's common grace and the particularity shown in becoming incarnate at a certain time, among a particular people, in the historical Jesus, who is at the same time the universal Saviour and Cosmic Christ.

I use this term 'Cosmic Christ' in a completely biblical sense, following the apostle Paul's understanding of Jesus not simply as Jewish Messiah, but as universal Lord, whose redemptive work was cosmic, embracing the whole created order (Ephesians 1: 9–10, 21–23; 3:7–11; 4:8–10; Colossians 1:15–20). It is to this Pantocrator (Revelation 1:8), the Cosmic Saviour and Lord, that every knee shall bow, in heaven, on earth and under the earth (Philippians 2:6–11), for the whole cosmos is created, sustained and redeemed by him. There is a distinction, but no contradiction, in the New Testament, between the human Jesus and the Cosmic Christ. They are one and the same Lord of all. It is of this scriptural Cosmic Christ that this chapter speaks.

We may feel this tension when we say that we are both human and Christian, which means that our attitude is universal and our faith commitment is particular. But this particularity—which is our commitment to Jesus, is not fundamentalist or exclusive. It should make us *more* human, *more* open, *more* universal.

In the chapter headed 'Universal Yearning' we discussed the Perennial Philosophy, and spoke of it as the soil in which all the great faiths have taken root. It has become increasingly clear to me, as I have lived through decades of my Christian life, that there are many people of other faiths and none, who participate in some way in the healing love of God.

Some of them consciously follow a mystical or religious path with their hearts open to compassion. Others manifest such compassion, but do not, for various reasons, affirm a particular faith. The Church itself has often brought about such a situation, for it has so misrepresented the compassionate, non-violent, healing Jesus, and projected such a negative and exclusive image of God that many sensitive and discerning people have turned away, thinking that this was the only God on offer. John Stott states the problem baldly:

> *How is it, I ask myself, that the Christian conscience not only approved but actually glamorized those terrible medieval Crusades as a Christ-glorifying form of mission, so that European Christian knights in shining armour rode forth to recover the holy places from Islam by force? It was an unholy blunder which Muslims have never forgotten, let alone forgiven, and which continues to obstruct the evangelization of the Muslim world, especially in the Middle East. Or how it is that torture could ever have been employed in the name of Jesus to combat heresy and enforce orthodoxy, so that the thumbscrews were turned on some miserable dissident until he capitulated? One might almost characterize it 'evangelization by torture', and that in the name of the Prince of Peace... Again, how is it that the cruel degradations of slavery and of the slave trade were not abolished in the so-called Christian West until 1800 years after Christ? Or how is it that racial prejudice and environmental pollution have become widely recognized as the evils they are only since the Second World War?*[1]

Since the watershed change in the fourth century, when the Emperor Constantine adopted Christianity as the state religion and perverted the meaning of the cross from suffering non-violence to a symbol of political and military power, the Church has been equivocal in its stance towards establishment, warfare, state affiliation and temporal gain.

This has marked the Orthodox churches of the East as well as the Latin churches of the West, and applies to the Roman as well as the Reformed traditions.

We are caught up on every side by global thinking in our own day, and it is significant that in 1993 there was a meeting of 250 world religious leaders at the parliament of religions in Chicago, and they signed 'The Declaration of a Global Ethic', drafted by the Swiss theologian Hans Küng. In the context of international violence, ecological pollution and human alienation, the document says: 'We affirm that a common set of core values is found in the teaching of the religions and that these form the basis of a global ethic.'[2]

The religious element in this declaration is that it is not in a legalistic framework that such a statement is made, but it advocates a spiritual transformation, and is oriented towards reflection, meditation, prayer and conversion of heart.

This does not encourage a facile ecumenism or a syncretistic compromise of the particular 'scandal' of the Christian revelation. But it does encourage us, with a new openness of mind and heart, to a dialogue of shared study, prayer and action that is open to the universal Spirit of God.

Historical Jesus & Cosmic Christ

It is in such a contemporary context that we must work out our attitude and action. We shall go on to talk about action, but the matter of our own attitude toward ourselves, our fellow-Christian and our global neighbours is vitally important as we ask ourselves how the perfect will of God is spelled out in our personal and corporate lives.

I have found, in my own experience, that the more I relate to people of other faiths or to honest humanists who have become friends and fellow-pilgrims, the more I find myself rooted in the historical Jesus, revealed to us in the New Testament, and in the Church at its best. I believe that Jesus died for all, and that if Christians, Buddhists, Hindus, Sikhs, Muslims or humanists are among the saved in the last day, they are there because of the grace of God manifest in Jesus. And in that day there will be a universal recognition of the cosmic nature of his person and work, and that he is truly the Saviour of the world.

This makes me more open to dialogue, more willing to listen, to learn, to share and to rejoice with those of other faiths, and also more eager and enthusiastic to share the treasure of the gospel in a humble manner.

What I say about the Cosmic Christ is that before Jesus of Bethlehem appeared on earth, the Cosmic Christ (the *Logos* of John's Gospel) was universally active in the created order, in the history of Israel, and wherever people sought for a religious and mystical dimension to their lives.

In Jesus, this Cosmic Christ became incarnate and accomplished the work of healing, redemption and reconciliation that has cosmic implications, and the consequences of which are the salvation and transformation of the world.

My own faith and practice is that I believe that in Jesus of Nazareth, the Word (*Logos*), the Cosmic Christ, took flesh for our salvation. I own him as Saviour, friend and brother, and experience an intimate relationship with him in love and prayer.

The witness of Paul, which declares both my vocation and my yearning, is found in Galatians 2:19–20: 'I have been crucified with Christ; and it is no longer I who live, but it is Christ who lives in me. And the life I now live in the flesh I live by faith in the Son of God, who loved me and gave himself for me.'

I also believe that this same Jesus is risen and glorified and, as the Cosmic Christ, communicates by the Holy Spirit with men and women universally. And in him, by the Holy Spirit, I am carried with all the people of God, into ultimate and intimate union with the Father, and within the dynamic mystery of the Holy Trinity.

Exclusivism, inclusivism, pluralism

It is not simply a matter of getting our doctrine right, but getting our 'believing and behaving' according to the will of God. There are times when I have been willing, in seeking to be pastorally right, to be theologically wrong. But in the last analysis I cannot believe that holds. If, for the sake of being gently sympathetic to a penitent, I risk being in the wrong doctrinally, I have to ask serious questions about my theology. I am very aware that for the sake of dogmatic rightness, the Church has indulged in inhuman and cruel practices. It is not that God changes his character throughout the epochs of history, but that our apprehension and awareness of the nature of God must undergo progressive purification. As Michael Ramsey said: 'God is Christlike, and in him is no un-Christlikeness at all.'[3]

The Church of England Synod Report *Towards a Theology for Inter-Faith Dialogue*[4] described three attitudes which may be adopted by various groups of Christians. Clear-cut categories do not always take account of various overlapping nuances, but they can be useful to map out an area and see things in wider perspective. We can then ask ourselves pertinent questions as to our own attitude, both to the evolving tradition and towards the expectations of people of goodwill outside our own faith. The three categories are as follows:

> *Exclusivism.* This attitude indicates the historic view that salvation cannot be found in other religions, but only in the Christian faith. Such a view used to be common among pre-Vatican II Roman Catholics, and is currently held in the conservative sections of evangelicalism.

> *Inclusivism.* This view would include all moral and sincere people of other faiths among the saved, but would usually affirm that the basis of their salvation is not good works or merit but the person and work of Christ. They would be secret or anonymous Christians, at least in this life. This is the position of Vatican II, and of many contemporary theologians and Christians.

Pluralism. This third view, in defining its position, often rejects exclusivism as presumptuous and arrogant, and inclusivism as patronizing or condescending. It does not hold the uniqueness of Christ, and gives equal and independent validity to the other world faiths. The idea that Christ might divide as well as unite is abhorrent to pluralists, and they are moved towards a syncretism that makes all religions different paths that lead to the top of the mountain.

Alister McGrath makes an objective evaluation of these three approaches.[5] His introductory description runs:

> *Three broad approaches can be identified: exclusivism, which holds that only those who hear and respond to the Christian gospel may be saved; inclusivism, which argues that, although Christianity represents the normative revelation of God, salvation is nonetheless possible for those who belong to other religious traditions; and pluralism, which holds that all religious traditions of humanity are equally paths to the same core of religious reality.*

Such categorization does ignore varying degrees and shades of opinion and it is interesting to find an ecumenical author like F.C. Happold writing in his *Mysticism*:

> *While I am reluctant to apply to Christianity such concepts as 'final' and 'truer than', since neither can be logically demonstrated as valid (they partake of the truth of faith, rather than of the truth of reason), I do, for reasons which will become apparent to the reader, recognize in Christianity a quality of 'uniqueness', something which I do not find in any of the other higher religions.[6]*

I have Christian friends who would ally themselves with one or other of all three categories, and the glory of the Anglican comprehensive tradition is also its pain, in that all three categories are represented both in breadth and depth. One of the sad (though humorous) things is, that although we would expect a certain dogmatic and exclusive mindset among the first group, I have found that some professing liberals among the pluralists are more arrogant than the exclusivists, and demand that you be as liberal as they!

There are, nevertheless, warm-hearted and loving people in all three groups, and I can imagine that the committed and sympathetic Mother Teresa of Calcutta, who is now in the nearer presence of our Lord, would have been doctrinally an exclusivist, and yet the love of God overflowed in her heart and life—because Christ possessed her.

If the human heart is centred upon Christ, then the mystical life of Christ will flow through the believer and into the world. That life will manifest itself in commitment to the values of love, and that means a life of compassion. 'Just as I have loved you,' said Jesus, 'you also should love one another. By this everyone will know that you are my disciples, if you have love for one another' (John 13:34–35). This is the only valid and genuine mark of a Christian.

COMMITMENT
& COMPASSION

Commitment and compassion are two words which indicate the shape of our lives in terms of surrender to Christ within the fellowship of the Church, and the spelling out of that commitment in a mind and heart dedicated to compassion.

There is, in this statement, the tension of believing in the uniqueness of God's revelation in Christ, together with a complete openness to men and women simply because they share our humanity. I'm reminded of the words of the Roman poet Terence: 'I am a human being; therefore nothing that is human is alien to me.'

Commitment

We have to ask where our basic commitment lies, and if it is compatible with compassion. In my own case I am Christ's man. I have been so, consciously, since the age of twelve years, when I was graced with a personal encounter, and recognized him as my Saviour, friend and brother. But I must also add that I feel a powerful response to God's words in Jeremiah 1:5: 'Before I formed you in the womb I knew you, and before you were born I consecrated you'.

I have been so dazzled by the light of Christ that all other lights (and I do acknowledge the reality and validity of other great teachers and faiths) either reflect aspects of the hidden Christ, or dim before the glory which shines from his transfigured person. It is as if I became drunk with Christ in that first encounter and, drinking of the wells of the Holy Spirit along the way, I have remained inebriated with gospel joy (Acts 2:13; Ephesians 5:18).

The source of my knowledge of Christ is primarily the New Testament record. The reality of the living Christ is continually mediated through the reading and exposition of scripture, the communion of the body and blood of Christ in the eucharist, and my liturgical and personal life of prayer. All this is within the context of the fellowship of the teaching Church and the communion of saints.

But as I have matured and progressed and been exposed to light and truth shining in other faiths I have found Christ hidden in all manner of places. I remember in my first year as a theological student, joining with a few other students one Sunday evening at the home of the dean of the theological faculty. He sat at the piano and suggested we sing some hymns.

One of the fellows suggested a hymn by a blind Scottish hymn-writer, George Matheson, 'Gather us in'. The dean looked at him severely over his half-moon spectacles and said: 'I meant a Christian hymn!' I think his real reply was tongue-in-cheek, but we did not sing it. I looked at it then, and I look at it now, remembering Matheson's wholehearted dedication to Christ, and I see it in a beautiful (though perhaps dated) expression of the consummation of all things in Christ, according to Ephesians 1:8–10:

> With all wisdom and insight he has made known to us the mystery of his will, according to his good pleasure that he set forth in Christ, as a plan for the fulness of time, to gather up all things in him, things in heaven and things on earth.

Matheson's hymn embraces the insights of Hinduism, Buddhism, Zoroastrianism, Confucianism, Taoism and Islam. However, it is not a sentimental and sloppy syncretism, but a true synthesis in the glory of the Cosmic Christ:

> Gather us in, thou love that fillest all;
> Gather our rival faiths within thy fold.
> Rend each man's temple-veil and bid it fall,
> That we may know that thou has been of old;
> Gather us in!
>
> Gather us in: We worship only thee;
> In varied names we stretch a common hand;
> In diverse forms a common soul we see;
> In many ships we seek one spirit-land;
> Gather us in!

Each sees one colour of thy rainbow-light,
Each looks upon one tint and calls it heaven;
Thou art the fullness of our partial sight;
We are not perfect till we find the seven;
Gather us in!

Thine is the mystic life great India craves,
Thine is the Parsee's sin-destroying beam,
Thine is the Buddhist's rest from tossing waves,
Thine is the empire of vast China's dream;
Gather us in!

Thine is the Roman's strength without his pride,
Thine is the Greek's glad world without its graves,
Thine is Judaea's law with love beside,
The truth that censures and the grace that saves;
Gather us in![1]

When I speak of the Cosmic Christ, I am not referring to some concept outside the New Testament. Both in the Christ-mysticism of John,[2] and of Paul,[3] we have a cosmic and universal *Pantocrator* in the book of Revelation.[4] He it is who gathers the universal fruits of his salvation, and offers them finally and in consummation to the Father, who is ultimately 'all in all'. (1 Corinthians 15:28)

In an exciting chapter entitled 'Christo-Mysticism', F.C. Happold reveals a breadth of vision which enhances our understanding of the Christ in relation to insights of other faiths:

Christo-mysticism has similarities with the bhakti-mysticism of the Gita and is akin to the mysticism of the Bodhisattva ideal of Mahayana Buddhism. It is a mysticism of loving faith in a Mediator between the naked Godhead and weak, suffering humanity. The key doctrine of Paul is that of the indwelling of the Spirit of the risen Christ, and this indwelling Spirit is intimately bound up in his mind with Christ crucified, with the man who died on a cross in time. For John and Paul, Jesus Christ is both the Life and the Life-giver, both the Revelation and the Revealer, both the Way and the Guide. In him are gathered into one things earthly and heavenly.[5]

Again, it is breathtaking to consider a theology which travels the boundaries of cosmic space, where our small earth is not at the centre of the universe, and in which the mysteries of God's relation with all that is not 'planet earth' is unknown to us. Alice Meynell, in her poem 'Christ in the Universe' spells this out. She speaks of our clear knowledge of the incarnation of God in Christ on earth, of the virgin birth, the ministry, crucifixion and resurrection of Jesus. No other planet has been told of such wonders, she says, and none can imagine the pain and bliss of such glories. Then she continues:

> But in the eternities,
> Doubtless we shall compare together, hear
> A million other gospels, in what guise.
> He trod the Pleiades, the lyre, and the Bear.
>
> O, be prepared, my soul!
> To read the inconceivable, to scan
> The myriad forms of God those stars unroll
> When, in our turn, we show to them a Man.[6]

Yet although I take great delight in sharing similarities, insights, and a process of cross-fertilization with Hindus, Buddhists and Sikhs, and though I am intrigued by widening my horizons in considering possibilities and nonsenses suggested by orthodox and new age theologians,[7] my life-commitment is to the Christ of the New Testament, interpreted within the catholic/evangelical traditions of the Church.

At the same time, in the fellowship of the Church, and conferring with all men and women of goodwill, I seek to bring to bear a more human and Christlike pattern to our fallen and needy humanity. And that brings us to our second word, compassion.

Compassion

I have quoted Michael Ramsey's famous remark 'God is Christlike, and in him is no un-Christlikeness at all'. These are the words which inspired John Taylor's book *The Christlike God*.[8] Its central thesis is that Jesus is the reflection, in a human life, of the being of God. It is the kind of book which every Christian should consider prayerfully, for it has a universal scope and reveals a personal and receptive attitude to other faiths, including an illuminating search into reflection upon the being of God before and outside the Christian tradition. Yet it is the Christlike God who is at the centre of John Taylor's study. To understand Christ as the revelation of God is the deepest and most wonderful discovery we can make, for it is we who are discovered in the search. The book must be taken whole, but its conclusion is breathtaking:

> *Thinking about God and loving God, thinking further and loving more, is a pendulum of wonder and incomprehension, illumination and darkness, loss and possession, abasement and bliss, which, once started, must continue for ever as we move on into the infinity of God. For all eternity we shall be travelling further and further into the knowledge and love of this God who is our home and our rest, and every step forward will bring us closer to everyone and everything that is included in God's love... to call him the Christlike God is the supreme truth we can ever learn about his nature and it certainly does not reduce him to our human scale or fit him into the small grasp of our finite apprehension. For God is the Beyond whom we recognize in all things but can never see or reach.*[9]

In the past, religious people of all faiths have compared and contrasted the best of their tradition with the worst of other traditions. This still happens, but must no longer be our practice. Over the last two decades I have been reading Jewish, Hindu, Sikh, Buddhist and Sufi texts,[10] and meeting and making friends of people of other faiths.

I have listened carefully, and shared with them not a watered-down version of the way of Christ, but a saving, loving, gospel Jesus, who is full of compassion. And that is the heart of the matter. My 'other-faith' friends have often been amazed at the compassionate Christ I have presented, for they have frequently known and experienced the image of God and Christ which the Church has projected, and the contrast has been stark.

It is not that I have presented an emasculated or sentimental Jesus who receives anyone, whatever their moral stance or dogmatic mind-set. Indeed, the kind of love that the biblical Christ reflects has steel in it! It is a penetrating and searching love that sears and burns unrighteousness and hypocrisy. The truth also is that there is often more reverence for the biblical Christ among some adherents of other faiths than among many nominal Christians.

I must admit, though, that many of the contemporary studies in inter-faith dialogue are not reaching many good and faithful Christians. Part of the problem, I think, is that many of these studies demand an intellectual challenge that is beyond the ability of many contemporary Christians—and they are also too busy.

I suppose you can argue that Christians, therefore, ought to stretch their minds and make time. But I noticed, standing next to John Taylor's book in the monastery library, a simpler book—no less profound and engaging. It was Henri Nouwen's *The Return of the Prodigal Son*.[11] This is not an intellectual book, but it is deeply moving and full of spiritual insight. It is one of Nouwen's last books and contains his reflections on that central story of God's compassion, the Prodigal Son (Luke 15:11–32).

Nouwen's inspiration for it was his encounter with Rembrandt's painting *The Return of the Prodigal Son*, and the book encapsulates the radiant love and mercy of God, manifested primarily in the Father, but operating at all levels of the story:

'Be compassionate just as your Father is compassionate.' That is the core message of the gospel. The way human beings are called to love one another is God's way. We are called to love another with the same selfless, outgoing love that we see in Rembrandt's depiction of the father. The compassion with which we are to love cannot be based upon a competitive life-style. It has to be this absolute compassion in which no trace of competition can be found. It has to be this radical love of enemy. If we are not only to be received by God, but also to receive God, we must become like the heavenly Father and see the world through his eyes.[12]

Compassion for all

Compassion. This is the very quality that some of my Buddhist friends tell me is missing in their observation of the lives of many Christians. The questionnaire, which was the basis of my book *My Questions—God's Questions*,[13] resulted in well over 300 questions. One, from a Buddhist friend, called into question the Christian attitude to the sacredness of life in the areas of human morality and towards animal life. In my reply, I spoke of the way in which, despite doctrinal differences, many Christians and Buddhists are learning from each other in these days, and I pointed out that it was my Christian commitment which led me to my pacifist stance of reconciliation as a human being, and to vegetarianism in my attitude to animal life. Then I said:

> There has been two-way traffic in this respect, for I still remember the powerful essay which Thomas Merton wrote during the Vietnam war, entitled 'Nhat Hanh is my Brother', affirming the bonds of a solidarity and brotherhood in a worldwide contemplative vision. It is strange to recall that Merton died in 1968 and that Thich Nhat Hanh continues to exercise a marvellous ecumenical ministry in Plum Village in France—teaching, writing, gardening and aiding refugees worldwide. The Hindu Ramakrishna Order was influenced by Christian social concern in its special blend of interior contemplation and humanitarian compassion. As we examine the roots of our spiritual traditions we find immense treasures, and these enable us to continue the process of cross-fertilization, which is the joy of our sharing.

Then, lest my Buddhist friend think that compassion was a virtue which Christians are now only becoming aware of, I quoted the description of 'A Compassionate Heart' by the seventh-century monk, Isaac of Syria:

> What is a compassionate heart? It is a heart on fire for the whole of creation, for humanity, for the birds, for the animals, for demons and all that exists. At the recollection and at the sight of them such a person's eyes overflow with tears owing to the vehemence of the compassion which grips his heart; as a result of his

deep mercy his heart shrinks and cannot bear to hear or look on
any injury, or the slightest suffering of anything in creation. This
is why he constantly offers up prayer full of tears, even for the ir-
rational animals and for the enemies of truth, even for those who
harm him, so that they may be protected and find mercy. He even
prays for the reptiles as a result of the great compassion which is
poured out beyond measure—after the likeness of God—in his
heart.[14]

It is clear that there is no exclusivism in Isaac of Syria's attitude, and he was wholly committed to Christ. It is because I am Christ's man that I have the ability, the confidence, the duty and the joy to aim at a universal compassion. I have not attained it, and certainly shall not attain it by my own effort—there is still too much of my fallen nature evident in my thinking. Christ's grace is as indispensable to holiness as it is to forgiveness—for they are both parts of the wholeness of salvation.

There are two main things this chapter has been saying. The first is that we must be wholly committed to Christ in life and death—though our vision will doubtless be greater than our performance! The second is that we must seek to live with compassion for all, while not becoming discouraged when our practice falls short of our vision. And for both we need the continued grace of God.

THE PERFECT WILL OF GOD

Readiness for God's will

In the final verse of his hymn, Charles Wesley wrote:

> *Ready for all Thy perfect will,*
> *My acts of faith and love repeat…*

If you had asked either of the Wesley brothers what was the perfect will of God, they would have quoted 1 Thessalonians 4:3: 'For this is the will of God, your sanctification', or an extended version on the theme:

> *I appeal to you therefore, brothers and sisters, by the mercies of God, to present your bodies as a living sacrifice, holy and acceptable to God, which is your spiritual worship. Do not be conformed to this world, but be transformed by the renewing of your minds, so that you may discern what is the will of God—what is good and acceptable and perfect. (Romans 12:1–2)*

The perfect will of God calls for the total dedication of all our human powers, body, mind and spirit, and their transformation by the fire of the Holy Spirit, until we are ablaze with the divine glory.

Our 'acts of faith and love' refer firstly to faith in God for salvation and sanctification, then love for God which overflows with a fervent desire to give ourselves in compassionate service in the world. The mystical life of faith and prayer which we have considered in these chapters cannot become a stagnant lake with no outlet. As 'faith without works is dead' so a life dedicated to God must overflow in forgiveness, joy and compassion among humankind. Otherwise it is an hypocrisy and, like a dammed-up stagnant lake, will produce decay and stench.

In our last chapter we used the word 'compassion', and it is the one quality which marks out a genuine religion from a religiosity which is either artificial or even demonic. The whole epistle of James witnesses to this, and makes the matter very clear:

> *Religion that is pure and undefiled before God the Father is this:*
> *to care for orphans and widows in their distress, and to keep one-*
> *self unstained by the world. (James 1:27)*

These words are even more specific in our own day, for human need is seen on a global scale, and 'the world' can now be understood in terms of the world systems which are dedicated to the pursuit of power, territory and material gain, and guilty of massive global, ecological pollution.

Even as I write I am conscious of the fact that I belong to a country which is one of the foremost in the arms trade. While bewailing the fact that we have just witnessed the race for nuclear capability between India and Pakistan, we possess Trident submarines with nuclear warheads, 'each submarine has a firepower several times more than the total firepower expended in the Second World War, and equivalent to at least one thousand Hiroshima bombs'.[1]

Sin can no longer be reckoned in terms of personal and parochial peccadilloes, but must be seen in a global context—social sin in which we all share, and have to bear responsibility.

To talk of the perfect will of God in such a context seems absurd. Our world is so out of kilter with God's intention that it is now evident as never before that the kingdom of God cannot be brought in as a result of human effort, whether religious or political. It can only come as the gift of God's miraculous intervention. Of course, that has always been the case, but our contemporary world dilemma is such that it has now become very clear.

If we did not believe that God's will for his world is reconciliation and compassion, then we would be in danger of despair. So, like many people today, we would either become cynical about any compassionate effort or movement, or be caught up in a compassion fatigue that would paralyse the springs of action.

The perfect will of God is the ultimate manifestation of his kingdom, and that will come by his grace and in his time. But meanwhile, we must be ready for that perfect will and give ourselves totally to show signs of its presence in the place where God has set us.

Some of us may find ourselves in places of persecution and

terror, like John McCarthy, Terry Waite and Brian Keenan during their terrorist imprisonment in Beirut, or in prison for some twenty-three years, like Nelson Mandela under the evil apartheid regime of South Africa.

In all these cases, they allied themselves with what they knew of the will of God in the circumstances in which they found themselves—and the consequence was a manifestation of God's kingdom which itself may become global in its influence.

Through this book I have sought an attitude of openness and dialogue with the great world faiths, but it is also necessary to say that *all* the world faiths are liable to corruption, for power always corrupts when separated from the restraints and discipline of primary compassion.

Brian Keenan's book *An Evil Cradling*[2] is essential reading in coming to understand how religion and culture can be perverted both in the context of Islam and Christianity, and how sinfulness must be seen in its national, international and religious manifestations. Keenan writes of the violence of his Muslim captors which is fed both by a perversion of religion that many Muslims would be ashamed of, and by the American icon of Rambo as hero and exemplar:

> *The man unresolved in himself chooses, as men have done throughout history, to take up arms against his sea of troubles. He carries his Kalashnikov on his arm, his handgun stuck in the waistband of his trousers, a belt of bullets slung around his shoulders. I had seen so many young men thus attired in Beirut, their weapons hanging from them and glistening in the sun. The guns were symbols of potency. The men were dressed as caricatures of Rambo. Many of them wore a headband tied and knotted at the side above the ear, just as the character in the movie had done. It is a curious paradox that this Rambo figure, this All-American hero, was the stereotype which these young Arab revolutionaries had adopted. They had taken on the cult figure of the Great Satan they so despised and whom they claimed was responsible for all the evil in the world. Emulating Rambo, they would reconquer the world and simultaneously rid themselves of that inadequacy which they could never admit.*

Before he was captured, Keenan had gone to a Beirut cinema showing a war film, set in Vietnam. Its story was not a story—it was about men killing one another with no purpose, and there was no meaningful exploration of the war, or of the inhumanity of it. His description is chilling:

> We sat there in the darkened cinema and as each character pulled out his weapon and began firing furiously, the young Arab men around us would groan and moan in a kind of ecstasy, crying out the names of the weapons. All around us in the cinema we could hear the words 'Kalashnikov, Kalashnikov; Beretta, Beretta.' These young men knew the names of every type of gun, even the names of mortars and rocket launchers. The cinema rang with a chant of excited worship.[3]

He then describes the way in which religion can be harnessed to evil ends, and how easy it is for prayer to God/Allah to become hysterical channels towards mindless violence:

> The cotton sheet that separated us from our captives also allowed us a deeper insight into their minds and their behaviour. Every morning before dawn, Said would come and sit at the other side of the sheet with a portable cassette player and would play a tape of some holy man chanting and reciting the Suras of the Koran. The tape would be loud and blaring. Said would sit chanting in unison with his mullah and after hours of this would become delirious. He would begin sobbing, then wailing. This self-induced morbidity seemed interminable. At times he would continue in this distraught and mind-jarring state literally for hours, and when he had finished another guard came. Said made his men pray, and they, like him, would work themselves up into a grief-stricken hysteria. Having to sit listening to this three times a day, day after day, was maddening. It was a kind of psychological torture.[4]

Keenan draws together the violence of his Muslim captors and their obsession with the culture and militarism of the West and writes ironically:

> Often [John McCarthy and I] talked about how the violence of men like our guards was at least partly conditioned by the glut of

*American video violence and how their twisted, obsessional con-
cern with sexuality was in part a response to the slew of nudity in
the Western films they saw. In our own way, we were subject to a
violence and perversion conditioned by products of the West. We
remembered how the guns that they had shown us were all of
European manufacture.*[5]

It serves no ecumenical purposes for a Christian to be silent about
the violence and evil found in the dark aspects of other religions,
and it is the duty of good Jews, Muslims, Buddhists, Sikhs and so
on to be open and honest about the sins of established Christianity,
like the violent conflicts between Christians in Northern Ireland, or
the Serbian Orthodox persecution of Muslims. The books of John
McCarthy, Terry Waite and Brian Keenan were themselves witnesses
to truth, justice, peace and compassion—prophetic witnesses in a
dark world.

From Brian Keenan, let us look at the experience and outcome
of the oppression of Nelson Mandela as a Christian victim of a
'Christian' state, which justified by scripture and theology the evils
of apartheid. 'Apartheid was a new term but an old idea,' says
Mandela;

*It literally means 'apartness', and it represented the codification
in one oppressive system of all the laws and regulations that had
kept Africans in an inferior position to whites for centuries. What
had been more or less de facto was to become relentlessly de jure.
The often haphazard segregation of the past three hundred years
was to be consolidated into a monolithic system that was diabolic
in its detail, inescapable in its reach and overwhelming in its
power.*[6]

When he appeared before Judge de Wet in the 1964 trial, Mandela
at one point laid aside his prepared speech and turned to face the
judge. The courtroom became extremely quiet as he spoke:

*During my lifetime I have dedicated myself to this struggle of the
African people. I have fought against white domination. I have
cherished the ideal of a democratic and free society in which all
persons live together in harmony and with equal opportunities. It*

*is an ideal which I hope to live for and to achieve. But if needs be,
it is an ideal for which I am prepared to die.*[7]

If ever a manifestation of the will of God was personified in a dedicated man it was in Nelson Mandela in those days. His own Christian faith was in the Wesleyan tradition, and it is worth setting out John Wesley's letter, which was written a few days before his death, to the young William Wilberforce in 1791, followed by Nelson Mandela's powerful witness in our own day. Wesley wrote:

Unless the Divine Power has raised you up to be as Athanasius, contra mundum, *I see not how you can go through your glorious enterprise in opposing that execrable villainy which is the scandal of religion, of England, and of human nature. Unless God has raised you up for this very thing, you will be worn out by the opposition of men and devils; but if God be for you, who can be against you? Are all of them together stronger than God? Oh, be not weary in well doing. Go on, in the name of God and in the power of his might, till even American slavery, the vilest that ever saw the sun, shall vanish away before it.*

Reading this morning a tract wrote by a poor African, I was particularly struck by that circumstance that a man who has a black skin, being wronged or outraged by a white man, can have no redress; it being a law in our colonies that the oath of a black man against a white goes for nothing. What villainy is this! That He who has guided you from your youth up may continue to strengthen you in this and in all things is the prayer of, Your affectionate Servant, John Wesley.[8]

...and the flame of Wesleyan fire which still burns in Nelson Mandela:

I never lost hope that this great transformation would occur. Not only because of the great heroes I have already cited, but because of the courage of the ordinary men and women of my country. I always knew that deep down in every heart there was mercy and generosity. No one is born hating another person because of the colour of his skin, or his background, or his religion. People must learn to hate, and if they can learn to hate, they can be taught to love, for love comes more naturally to the human heart than its opposite. Even in the grimmest times in prison, when my comrades and I were pushed to our limits, I would see a glimmer of humanity in one of my guards, perhaps just for a second, but it was enough to reassure me and keep me going. Man's goodness is a flame that can be hidden but never extinguished.[9]

If we read these experiences in the light of the passage we quoted from Romans 12, it will be clear that readiness for the perfect will of God is spelled out in our own imperfect and impossible situations. But it is also clear that within the dilemma of the human condition, in all its shame and glory, the light and fire of God's Holy Spirit is at work, purging, refining, transforming.

The demand is that body, mind and spirit are dedicated to God in our lowly or exalted human situations—teaching in a school, running an Amnesty International group, caring for Aids victims, on the road as a traffic warden, selling the *Big Issue* as unemployed and homeless, or as a member of British or European Parliament.

My own hermit perspective sometimes makes me feel kinship with the lonely, the terminally ill and the dying, especially during my early morning hours of prayer in the darkness. And sometimes I feel the glory, ecstasy and contemplative wonder of the great saints in glory. You must see your own situation as reflecting both the dilemma and wonder of being human, reaching out a hand of forgiveness and compassion, in both personal and communal loving service.

I was living in solitude in my caravan in November 1991 when Terry Waite was at last released, and having spent a long time in prayer and longing for the Beirut hostages, the news was like a source of the divine fire on a cold, bleak day. My joy in sharing is evident in what I wrote then:

I write on a grey but a splendid day. It has rained all night and at 5.45 a.m. going up to do the chickens was the darkest and muddiest for weeks. It continues to pour with rain and the caravan is trembling in the wind.

But it is a splendid, a glorious day because Terry Waite was released last evening after 1763 days of captivity. He and Tom

Sutherland are free, and are talking about the release of hostage Terry Anderson and the other Americans who are left. I have pictures of Brian Keenan, John McCarthy, Jackie Mann and Terry Waite on my wall and they have been woven into my crying and praying through all the months of my solitude. And now they are all free!

I know it is not just my prayer, but my prayers have been part of the warp and woof of the pattern of yearning, longing, sympathy, compassion, empathy. I've been considering those words—entering into, taking upon and within oneself the pain, the suffering, the feeling, the yearning for freedom, for release, for healing. This is my work, my pain, my glory. And it is not just mine, but everyone's. [10]

DEATH & GLORY

Our people die well

People's faces always light up when I tell them that John Wesley said 'Our people die well'. I go on to tell of a painting in a large gilt frame that I saw when I was a boy. It portrayed a deathbed scene which was full of glory! A white-bearded old man was propped up in an ample bed with pillows, but his arms were extended, his eyes raised heavenwards, and a shaft of light fell upon his face, irradiating it with beauty and anticipation. His friends were kneeling and standing about his bed in prayer, and the caption under the picture read: 'A Methodist Deathbed'.

So when I read, in later years, John Wesley's words, it made me laugh with joy. The early Methodists not only rejoiced in the assurance of sins forgiven, and the awareness of the sanctifying Holy Spirit, but they lived in anticipation of future glory, and their joy overflowed into the experience of death, carrying the believer into heaven.

Charles Wesley did not speak lightly of death as the sealing of God's endless mercies, and it is reassuring for us to know that both brothers' deaths exemplified their faith in the risen Lord of life and death.

Charles died in 1788 at the age of eighty-one years, and one of those who cared for him spoke of his 'solid hope and unshaken confidence in Christ, which kept his mind in perfect peace'.[1] Just days before his death he wrote these words:

> *In age and feebleness extreme*
> *Who shall a sinful soul redeem?*
> *Jesus, my only hope Thou art,*
> *Strength of my failing flesh and heart:*
> *O could I catch a smile from Thee,*
> *And drop into Eternity!*

And he did!

At the time, his brother John, at eighty-five years of age, was on a preaching tour, and he heard of the news in Bolton. Such news moved him deeply, and he stood in the chapel pulpit and read out the first verse of his brother's beautiful hymn on the story of wrestling Jacob.[2] When he came to the words 'My company before is gone, And I am left alone with thee' he broke down and wept in public for the first time in fifty years' ministry. He burst into a flood of tears, sat down in the pulpit, and covered his face with his hands. This was no failure of faith, but an expression of brotherly love and profound affection that had bound the brothers together all their lives. Like his Saviour at the grave of Lazarus, he wept, and if we weep in bereavement over a loved one, such tears are precious, and rich in sorrow and love.

John continued proclaiming the Jesus he loved, but in 1791, at eighty-eight years of age, his time came. After he had written his supportive letter to the young William Wilberforce, he returned to his rooms in City Road London, and, without pain or distress, his life began to ebb away, and his friends surrounded him with love and support. Just three days before he died, in a clear voice, he repeated a verse from one of his brother's hymns:

> *Till glad I lay this body down,*
> *Thy servant, Lord, attend;*
> *And O! My life of mercy crown*
> *With a triumphant end.*

I must admit that my gilt-framed Victorian picture of a Methodist deathbed may have been somewhat sentimental—yet it touched the heart of the boy I was then. But there is no mistaking the fact that both the Wesley brothers loved our Lord in life, entered into his nearer presence at death, and called forth this positive evaluation by John's biographer:

Death came to Wesley with no fears, no ugliness. His calm soul was ready, nor was there any doubt or shadow or vain reproach in the mind of this holy man. The men and women who reverently stood or knelt in his room saw the supreme reward of one who lived in the light of truth. 'Sir,' said one of them, 'we are come to rejoice with you.' With such reverence, and such a conviction of

triumph, men have watched the last moments of saints or philoso-
phers, disciples have listened eagerly to the last words of those al-
most in sight of the opening heavens. [3]

Death was the seal on the endless mercies of God manifested in the personal faith, public proclamation, and social witness[4] of the Wesley brothers.

The communion of saints

We have spoken about mystical touches of God in the experience of many people, and the fact that they are often not spoken about because they are personal or sacred, or because of the danger of ridicule. The more I have shared such experiences in retreats and conferences, the more people have been forthcoming about their own glimpses of intuition in nature-mysticism or moments of glory as they have been touched by the mystery of God.

During one retreat I conducted at Cropthorne, Pershore, one woman spoke of the death of her mother some years before, which had left a lasting impression upon her own life. Her mother's sister (let's call her Lucy), had died previously, and now her mother was dying. At one moment, the retreatant related, her mother sat up in bed, opened her eyes wide, and said: 'Oh, you've come, Lucy—and who are all those lovely people with you?' And she lay back, closed her eyes, and died.

The retreatant did not see anything herself, but was convinced then, and affirms ever since, that her mother entered into the company of the blessed—which we call the communion of saints.

I have always believed in the nearness of our brothers and sisters in Christ who are part of his Church on the further side of death. We sometimes make distinctions like:

The Church militant (on earth)

The Church expectant (in the nearer presence of Christ)

The Church triumphant (the great saints in glory)

But there is only one Church, and how wonderfully Charles Wesley glimpses its unity and glory:

> *One family we dwell in him,*
> *One church, above, beneath,*
> *Though now divided by the stream,*
> *The narrow stream of death:*
> *One army of the living God,*
> *To his command we bow;*
> *Part of his host have crossed the flood,*
> *And part are crossing now.*[5]

It is a hymn worth learning, and it underlines the communal aspect of the saints in glory and their fellowship with us. We are not meant to think of heaven in an egotistical, individualistic way, for the New Testament emphasizes its communal aspect as a feast, a festal gathering, a communion of saints in light and glory, with a profound participation and inter-penetration into the nature of God that we have scarcely begun to conceive here on earth.

Yet there is also the deeply personal dimension of glory in and beyond death, as Paul expressed the tension: 'I am hard pressed between the two: my desire is to depart and be with Christ, for that is far better; but to remain in the flesh is more necessary for you' (Philippians 1:23–24).

There is a hymn from Wesley's 1779 collection which is intensely personal, and at the same time expresses the tremendous communal joy and welcome of heaven. Set to the beautiful Welsh tune *Trewen*[6] it speaks of the joy of a brother or sister who has been freed from finitude and mortality into the joy and glory of heaven. The second verse contrasts the storms and tempests of the companions left behind, sailing on life's fitful waters, with the assurance, rest and peace of the believer who has gone before. The final verse portrays the shouting triumph of the whole ship's company (a lovely image for the communion of saints!) when the Saviour brings the vessel into harbour, and together they rejoice in the ecstatic welcome of heaven:

> *Rejoice for a brother deceased,*
> *Our loss is his infinite gain;*
> *A soul out of prison released,*
> *And freed from its bodily chain:*

With songs let us follow his flight,
And mount with his spirit above,
Escaped to the mansions of light,
And lodged in the Eden of love.

Our brother the haven has gained,
Outflying the tempest and wind,
His rest he has sooner obtained,
And left his companions behind,
Still tossed on a sea of distress
Hard toiling to make the blest shore,
Where all is assurance and peace,
And sorrow and sin are no more.

There all the ship's company meet
Who sailed with the Saviour beneath,
With shouting each other they greet,
And triumph o'er trouble and death:
The voyage of life's at an end,
The mortal affliction is passed;
The age that in heaven they spend,
For ever and ever shall last.[7]

I don't see why the departed believer may not, by God's grace, share in some of the joy of a Christian funeral (Luke 9:30–31),[8] so I look forward to participating from the glory side—and I hope this hymn may be sung!

The kingdom of heaven

The word eschatology means 'the last things' and has to do with death and judgment, and with the kingdom of glory, in which believers and the whole cosmos will be transfigured. The nineteenth-century liberals used to think of the kingdom of God as a moral ideal which is the reward of human effort and which can be realized as the leaven of religious teaching works through society. The two World Wars, the horrors of the Soviet archipelagos and the Nazi Holocaust have made it very clear that degradation and sinfulness have become woven into our very nature. I call two theological witnesses to this desperate situation. The first is John Macquarrie:

> When we do look at actual human existing, we perceive a massive disorder in existence, a pathology that seems to extend all through existence, whether we consider the community or the individual, and that stultifies it. Because of this prevalent disorder, the potentialities of existence are not actualized as they might be, but are lost or stunted or distorted.[9]

The second is Alister McGrath:

> [There is] a general collapse in confidence in human civilization as a means of bringing the kingdom of God to fulfilment. World War I was an especially traumatic episode in this respect. The Holocaust, the development of nuclear weapons and the threat of nuclear war, and the continuing threat to the destruction of the environment through human exploitation of its resources, have all raised doubts concerning the credibility of the vision of liberal humanist forms of Christianity.[10]

This expresses what theologians call 'the Fall', and we can think of the problem like this:

Falling short; or failing to reach the standard of righteousness;

Falling down; or failing to be people of moral integrity;

Falling from; or failing to live in relationships of love;

Falling away; or losing our rootedness and stability in God.

We who are made in God's image have allowed that image to become distorted, cracked, broken, perverted by sin, and the result is that we have fallen from an integrating love in our own persons, and therefore in our relationships, and have become lost to ourselves and to God.

The saving gospel of Christ reconciles us to God and to one another through forgiveness, restoration and the gift of the Holy Spirit, in order that the image of God may be restored in us as individuals and as a community of love. This begins in our being converted to God by grace and being progressively sanctified in holiness by the work of the Holy Spirit. But it is quite clear that we cannot bring in this kingdom of love and holiness by our own efforts—we need God's salvation.

This word salvation, as we have seen, is not merely a 'save your soul' matter. It means the restoration of the whole person, and it means that we show the evidence of faith in our daily lives, both on a personal and a social level.

It also has an eschatological dimension—that of eternity. We are made by and for God, and we must begin experiencing our salvation here and now, and know its consummation in heaven. When Jesus came in his incarnation, he brought heaven with him, so that eschatology begins in my soul, in my family, in my neighbourhood and spreads out through the whole world.

There have been different ways of understanding eschatology. In his section on the 'Last Things' McGrath lays out three possibilities:

1. *Futurist:* The kingdom of God is something which remains in the future, and will intervene disruptively in the midst of human history.

2. *Inaugurated:* The kingdom of God has begun to exercise its influence within human history, although its full realization and fulfilment lie in the future.

3. *Realized:* The kingdom of God has already been realized in the coming of Jesus.[11]

In the first, futurist view, the danger is that we put off the reality of God's living, loving presence and power to some heaven which does not impinge on our personal and social lives—'pie in the sky when you die'.

In the third, realized view, the entire concentration on the present keeps your eyes on the ground, and loses a sense of the goal, the consummation and the completion of our whole salvation in the glory of heaven.

That leaves us with the second, inaugurated view, which means that Jesus did bring the kingdom—planted, initiated and inaugurated it by his presence, forgiving, loving and miracles of healing. But he did not consummate it. He spoke of it as future expectation, and taught his disciples to look and pray 'your kingdom come', seeking it first in life's priorities.

His parables speak of the kingdom being planted, growing secretly and bearing harvest (Matthew 13:24–29, 31–32, 36–42). The invisible, hidden activity of the kingdom energies would work here and now, but would yield their full potential in the last day.

So there is a tension for Christians. They must live in the present experience of the love and joy of Christ in their hearts, allowing his compassion to be manifested in the world. But they must also keep their hearts and eyes in heaven, from whence our Lord will come. Paul gave himself in complete dedication in his daily life, allowing the power of Jesus to flow through him. But as he was nearing his death, he spoke for himself and for all Christians when he said:

> I have fought the good fight, I have finished the race, I have kept the faith. From now on there is reserved for me the crown of righteousness, which the Lord, the righteous judge, will give me on that day, and not only to me but also to all who have longed for his appearing. (2 Timothy 4:7–8)

The gift of the Holy Spirit is the key to the resolution of this tension of the 'now' and the 'not yet' of the kingdom. One of my favourite passages of Paul is Romans 8:18–27, where the whole wonder unfolds before our eyes. We are caught up in the personal and cosmic yearning of creation, feeling the birth-pangs of future glory.

The Spirit cries, groans and yearns within the created order, waiting, expecting and even receiving as a foretaste the joy of full redemption. Salvation is seen here in all its inclusive glory. Our souls are to be saved from all the bondage of sin and evil; our minds will be illumined with the fulness of understanding; our bodies will be transformed into immortality, and shine with resurrection glory. And all this will be in the context of the transfiguration of the whole universe.

It is clear why Charles Wesley spoke of death as the seal of God's endless mercies, for it was the entrance into the nearer presence of our Lord. The fire of the Holy Spirit which our hymn has celebrated is the kindling of the Holy Spirit, and that same Spirit is the pledge, the promise, the foretaste of our inheritance in heaven:

> *Finish then thy new creation,*
> *Pure and spotless let us be;*
> *Let us see thy great salvation,*
> *Perfectly restored in thee:*
> *Changed from glory into glory,*
> *Till in heaven we take our place,*
> *Till we cast our crowns before thee,*
> *Lost in wonder, love, and praise.* [12]

EPILOGUE

MAKE THE SACRIFICE
COMPLETE

I made a special journey this year, to deliver the annual Franciscan Lecture to our Pentecost General Chapter, meeting at our mother house in Dorset.

Brother Francis, our oldest friar, presided at the closing eucharist, with radiance and simplicity. I was filled with joy when all the friars sang, with great gusto, the last hymn, which was Wesley's 'O thou who camest from above'!

The words of John Wesley came to me as I looked around: 'If I had twelve who were wholly given to God, I would turn the world upside down'. So I prayed that this hymn would become a reality in our lives, and that the divine fire might burn upon the altar of our hearts, and draw those who were shivering in the cold and dark places of our world into its radiant light and warmth.

This is my prayer for you, as you come to the end of this book. You were created to be the temple of God in the world; you were meant to be aflame with his glory; you were shaped for God's indwelling and fiery joy.

So enter into your inheritance and claim what is yours today! Pray that the fire of God may fall and consume the sacrifice. Let your small flame join with others in the conflagration of divine love:

> *Ready for all Thy perfect will,*
> *My acts of faith and love repeat,*
> *Till death Thy endless mercies seal,*
> *And make the sacrifice complete.*

References

The flame of sacred love

1. Charles Wesley (1707–88), 1779 Collection, No. 327.

Evangelical conversion

1. See 'Come, Holy Ghost, all-quickening fire', *Hymns and Psalms* (Methodist Publishing House, 1983), No. 282.

2. See, for instance, William Law, *A Serious Call to a Devout and Holy Life*, 1729.

3. Cited in Albert C. Outler, *John Wesley* (OUP Inc. 1964), p. 66.

4. R.W. Gribben, 'John Wesley', in Gorden S. Wakefield (ed.), *A Dictionary of Christian Spirituality* (SCM Press, 1983), p. 395.

5. Cited in Kallistos Ware, *The Orthodox Way* (Mowbray, 1979), pp. 146–147

6. Augustine, *Confessions*, VIII, 12.

Catholic spirituality

1. See 'An Olive Branch to the Romans', Outler (*op. cit.*, pp. 492–499).

2. Thomas Merton, *The Seven Storey Mountain* (Harcourt Brace Inc., 1949).

3. Thomas Merton, 'The White Pebble', in *Where I Found Christ,* ed. John A. O'Brien (Doubleday, 1950), p. 234.

4. *Monastic Exchange*, Vol. 1, Spring, 1969, p. 87.

5. John Eudes Bamberger, 'A Homily', in *Continuum*, Vol. 7, No. 2, p. 260.

6. See Brother Ramon SSF, 'Contemplation in the World', in *Soul Friends* (Marshall Pickering, 1989).

7. Thomas Merton, *Raids on the Unspeakable* (New Directions, 1961), p. 33.

8. Brother Ramon SSF, *Deeper into God* (Marshall Pickering, 1987), p. 77.

9. Vincent of Lerins, *Commonitorium*, XXIII, 28.

Rooted in scripture

1. James Burns, *Hymns and Psalms*, No. 523.

2. Charles Wesley, *Hymns and Psalms*, No. 468.

3. Raymond E. Brown, *The Gospel According to John* (2 vols) (Doubleday, 1966). *An Introduction to the New Testament* (Doubleday, 1997).

4. John Macquarrie, *Principles of Christian Theology* (SCM Press, 1977).

5. Macquarrie, *op. cit.*, p. 8.

6. Macquarrie, *op. cit.*, p10.

7. For an account of the interpretation of scripture, see Alister McGrath, *Christian Theology* (Blackwell, 1994), pp. 174–182.

8. William Barclay, *Testament of Faith* (Mowbray, 1975), p. 103.

9. Charles Wesley, *Hymns and Psalms*, No. 469.

A disciplined life

1. Mirror of Perfection, 96, Marion A. Habig, St Francis of Assisi, Omnibus of Sources (SPCK, 1973), p. 1230.

2. John Ruysbroeck, *Adornment of Spiritual Marriage* (J.M. Dent), pp. 69–70.

3. *Grow with the Bible*, P.O. Box 176, Berkhamsted, UP4 3FM.

4. An address worth noting in this context is The National Retreat Association, 24 South Audley Street, London, W1Y 5DL, and its magazine, *Vision*.

5. See the excellent account of the Third Order in Omer Englebert, *St Francis of Assisi* (Burns & Oates, 1950), pp. 229ff. Also 'The Third Order' in Brother Ramon SSF, *Franciscan Spirituality* (SPCK, 1994), pp. 99–110.

The adventure of prayer

1. See 'The Jesus Prayer', in Brother Ramon SSF, *The Heart of Prayer* (Marshall Pickering, 1995), pp. 102–107.

2. The Prison Phoenix Trust provides for the teaching of meditation to prisoners. Information may be obtained from The Prison Phoenix trust, P.O. Box 328, Oxford, OX1 1PJ. I owe this exercise to the book offered to all prisoners who request it: Bo Lozoff, *We're All Doing Time* (Human Kindness Foundation, 1985), p. 91.

3. Brother Ramon SSF, *The Heart of Prayer*, *passim*.

4. Charles Wesley, 'O Love Divine', *The New English Hymnal* (The Canterbury Press, 1986), No. 424.

Universal yearning

1. I am indebted, in this chapter, to 'The Perennial Philosophy', in F.C. Happold, *Mysticism* (Harmondsworth: Penguin Books, 1963), pp. 18–21. Wider reading in this area may also be found in Aldous Huxley, *The Perennial Philosophy* (Collins, 1946), *passim*.

The mystery of God

1. Rudolf Otto, *The Idea of the Holy* (OUP, 1923).

2. See 'Mysticism', in Gordon S. Wakefield, *A Dictionary of Christian Spirituality* (SCM Press, 1983), pp. 272–274.

3. Happold, *op. cit.*, p. 19.

4. Clifton Wolters (trans.), *The Cloud of Unknowing* (Penguin Books, 1966).

5. Fritjof Capra, *The Tao of Physics* (1976); *The Turning Point* (1982) (both Fontana).

6. Capra, *The Tao of Physics*, p. 11.

7. Fritjof Capra, *The Web of Life* (Anchor, 1996).

8. Bede Griffiths, *A New Vision of Reality* (Collins, 1989).

9. Griffiths, *op. cit.*, p. 278.

10. Griffiths, *op. cit.*, p. 282.

The timeless moment

1. Frances Van Altyne, The Baptist Church Hymnal (Psalms & Hymns Trust, 1933), No. 383.

2. Michael Mayne, *This Sunrise of Wonder* (HarperCollins, 1995), p. 8.

3. Quoted from the Religious Experience Research Centre archives (No. 48), (Westminster College, Oxford).

4. The following three volumes, all published 1977 by The Religious Experience Research Unit, are recommended. They contain case histories and interviews:

    Edward Robinson, *The Original Vision: Religious Experience of Childhood* (Archive Account No. 57)

    Timothy Beardsworth, *A Sense of Presence: Visionary and Ecstatic Experience*

    Edward Robinson (ed), *This Time-Bound Ladder: Ten Dialogues on Religious Experience*

5. Robinson, *The Original Vision,* pp. 32–33.

6. Robinson, *The Original Vision,* p. 33.

7. Rosemary Sutcliffe, *Blue Remembered Hills* (Bodley Head, 1983), p. 132.

8. Cited in Happold, *op. cit.*, pp. 348–349.

9. J.W.N. Sullivan, *But for the Grace of God* (Jonathan Cape, 1932), p. 62.

10. Cited in Mayne, *op. cit.*, p. 37.

Mystical & prophetic religion

1. Thomas Merton, *Faith and Violence* (Univ. of Notre Dame Press, 1968), p. 219.

2. Within Islam the Sufi tradition affirms the immanence of God; in high Hinduism the unity of Brahman lies behind all the popular manifestation of the gods.

Guarding the fire

1. This poem can profitably be read in the context of Jacopone's mystical life and death. See Brother Ramon SSF, *Jacopone* (Collins, 1990), pp. 212–218.

2. See parts I and II of Brother Ramon SSF, *A Hidden Fire* (Marshall Pickering, 1985) and *The Heart of Prayer*, pp. 179–191.

3. Brother Ramon SSF, *The Prayer Mountain* (The Canterbury Press, 1998). This book shares the mystical teaching through the mountain peaks of scripture, while at the same time guarding the sacredness of the inner life of prayer.

4. Louis Fischer, *The Life of Mahatma Gandhi*, 1982.

5. John of the Cross, *The Living Flame of Love*, 4.17. Kieran Kavanagh, OCD (trans.), *The Collected Works of John of the Cross* (ICS Publications, 1979), p. 649.

6. Iain Matthew, *The Impact of God* (Hodder & Stoughton, 1985), pp. 23, 24. The poem translation is by Marjorie Flower OCD.

7. Matthew, *op. cit.*, pp. 24, 25.

8. Kavanagh (trans.), *op. cit.*, pp. 524, 525.

Light and fire

1. *Hymns and Psalms*, No. 457.

2. Symeon the New Theologian, *The Discourses* (trans. C.J. de Catanzaro), (Paulist Press, 1980).

3. de Catanzaro (trans.), *op. cit.*, pp. 245–246.

4. de Catanzaro (trans.), *op. cit.*, pp. 200–201.

5. de Catanzaro (trans.), *op. cit.*, p. 376.

6. Vladimir Lossky, *The Mystical Theology of the Eastern Church* (James Clarke, 1954), p. 222.

7. Cited in Lossky, *op. cit.*, p. 225.

8. Cited in Lossky, *op. cit.*, p. 219.

9. Kavanagh (trans.), *op. cit.*, p. 350.

The energies of love

1. Cited in George A. Maloney, *Gold, Frankincense and Myrrh* (Crossroad, 1977), pp. 71–72.

2. Maloney, *op. cit.*, pp. 69–70.

3. According to their preference for one 'sign' or the other, mystical writers may be characterized as either 'nocturnal' or 'solar'. Clement of Alexandria, Gregory of Nyssa and Dionysius the Areopagite give performance to the sign of darkness; Origen, Gregory the Theologian, Evagrius, the Homilies of Macarius, Symeon the New Theologian and Gregory Palamas use chiefly the sign of light. See Ware, *The Orthodox Way*, pp. 169–170.

4. William Johnston, *Mystical Theology* (HarperCollins, 1995), p. 82.

5. Johnston, *op. cit.*, p. 239.

6. Lossky, *op. cit.*, p. 69.

7. Lossky, *op. cit.*, p. 70.

8. Quoted in H.A. Hodges and A.M. Allchin, *A Rapture of Praise* (Hodder & Stoughton, 1966), p. 47.

The prayer of quiet

1. Lossky, *op. cit.*, p. 208.

2. Ware, *op. cit.*, p. 163.

3. Cited in Outler, *op. cit.*, p. 9.

4. Outler, *op. cit.*, pp. 9, 31, 119.

5. Maloney, *op. cit.*, p. 169.

6. Johnston, *op. cit.*, p. 76.

7. Brother Ramon SSF, *The Heart of Prayer*, pp. 102–107.

8. R.M. French (trans.), *The Way of the Pilgrim*, (SPCK, 1930).

9. Cited in Johnston, *op. cit.*, p. 77.

10. French, *op. cit.*, p. 32.

Christ-centred mysticism

1. John Stott, *The Contemporary Christian* (IVP, 1992), pp. 191–192.

2. Cited in Johnston, *op. cit.*, p. 297.

3. A.M. Ramsey, *God, Christ and the World* (SCM Press, 1969), p. 98.

4. Anglican Consultative Council, 1984.

5. McGrath, *op. cit.*, pp. 458–464.

6. Happold, *op. cit.*, p. 16.

Commitment and compassion

1. George Matheson, 'Gather Us In', *Psalms and Hymns*.

2. In the Prologue of the pre-Incarnate *Logos* (John 1:1–18), and in the vine and branches union of John 15:1–11. Dean

Inge, in his *Christian Mysticism* (Longmans Green & Co, 1907), calls John's Gospel 'the charter of Christian Mysticism'.

3. In the mystic vision of 2 Corinthians 12; the cosmic Christ of Colossians 1:9–20, 24–29; of Ephesians 1:3–10, and of Philippians 2:5–11.

4. Revelation 1:9–20. See Brother Ramon SSF, *The Listening Heart* (Marshall Pickering, 1996), pp. 16–22.

5. Happold, *op. cit.*, p. 165.

6. D.H.S. Nicholason (ed.), *The Oxford Book of English Mystical Verse* (OUP, 1917), pp. 463–464.

7. John Davidson, *The Gospel of Jesus* (Shaftesbury: Element, 1995)—of this book I would say beware of the gnosticism. While appreciating many of the creation-spirituality insights of Matthew Fox, there is a neglect and a negative attitude towards redemption-centred spirituality in his writings. He illustrates the danger of a concept of 'cosmic Christ' adrift from its scriptural base and the danger of subjective interpretation. See, for example, Matthew Fox, *The Coming of the Cosmic Christ* (Harper Inc., 1988).

8. John Taylor, *The Christlike God* (SCM Press, 1992).

9. Taylor, *op. cit.*, pp. 279–280.

10. See Bede Griffiths, *Universal Wisdom: A Journey through the Sacred Wisdom of the World* (HarperCollins, 1994).

11. Henri Nouwen, *The Return of the Prodigal Son* (Darton, Longman & Todd, 1994).

12. Nouwen, *op. cit.*, p. 126.

13. Brother Ramon SSF, *My Questions—God's Questions* (SPCK, 1998).

14. Cited in A.M. Allchin, *Heart of Compassion* (Darton, Longman & Todd, 1989), p. 9.

The perfect will of God

1. See Gerard W. Hughes, *Oh God, Why?* (The Bible Reading Fellowship, 1993), p. 91.

2. Brian Keenan, *An Evil Cradling* (Hutchinson, 1992).

3. Keenan, *op. cit.*, p. 133.

4. Keenan, *op. cit.*, p. 220.

5. Keenan, *op. cit.*, p. 289.

6. Nelson Mandela, *A Long Walk to Freedom* (Little, Brown, 1994), p. 404.

7. Mandela, *op. cit.*, p. 354. These words are from Nelson Mandela's defence before Judge de Wet in the 1964 Rivonia trial.

8. C.E. Vulliamy, *John Wesley* (Epworth Press, 1931), p. 348.

9. Mandela, *op. cit.*, p. 615.

10. Brother Ramon SSF, *Forty Days and Forty Nights* (Marshall Pickering, 1993), p. 192.

Death & glory

1. Vulliamy, *op. cit.*, p 162.

2. 'Come O thou Traveller unknown', *Hymns and Psalms,* No. 434.

3. Vulliamy, *op. cit.*, p. 348.

4. 'Wesley's influence upon the social, industrial and religious life of the eighteenth century in England has to be reckoned with as one of the prime historical factors of that period' (Vulliamy, *op. cit.*, p. vvi).

5. 'Come, let us join our friends above', *Hymns and Psalms*, No. 812.

6. *Hymns and Psalms*, No. 450, tune ii.

7. *Wesley's Hymns*, 1779, No. 49.

8. It is significant that Moses and Elijah talked with Jesus concerning his exodus on the Mount of Transfiguration (Luke 9:30–31).

9. Macquarrie, *op. cit.*, p. 69.

10. McGrath, *op. cit.*, p. 470.

11. McGrath, *op. cit.*, p. 470.

12. *Hymns and Psalms*, No. 267.

ACKNOWLEDGMENTS

William Barclay, *Testament of Faith*, Mowbray. Fritjof Capra, *The Tao of Physics*, Fontana. Extracts from *Symeon the New Theologian*, translation by C.J. deCatanzaro 1980 by the Missionary Society of St Paul the Apostle in the State of New York. Used by permission of Paulist Press Inc. *The Way of a Pilgrim*, R.M. French (Ed.), SPCK. Bede Griffiths, *A New Vision of Reality*, Collins. F.C. Happold, *Mysticism*, Penguin Books UK. William Johnston, *Mystical Theology*, HarperCollins. Extract from *The Collected Works of St John of the Cross* translated by Kieran Kavanagh and Otilio Rodriguez © 1979, 1991, by Washington Province of Discalced Carmelites. ICS Publications 2131 Lincoln Road N.E. Washington, DC 20002, USA. Brian Keenan, *An Evil Cradling*, published by Hutchinson. Vladimir Lossky, *The Mystical Theology of the Eastern Church*, published by James Clarke and Co., Ltd. Alister McGrath, *Christian Theology*, published by Blackwell Publishers. John Macquarrie, *Principles of Christian Theology*, SCM Press, 1977. George A. Maloney, *Gold, Frankincense and Myrrh*, the Crossroad Publishing Co. Inc. Nelson Mandela, *A Long Walk to Freedom*, published by Little, Brown and Co. UK. Iain Matthew, *The Impact of God*, copyright © 1985, reproduced by permission of Hodder & Stoughton. Michael Mayne, *This Sunrise of Wonder*, HarperCollins. Thomas Merton, *Faith and Violence*, University of Notre Dame Press. Thomas Merton, *Raids on the Unspeakable*, published by New Directions, Inc.. Thomas Merton, 'The White Pebble', in John A. O'Brien (Ed.), *Where I Found Christ*, Doubleday. Extract from *The Return of the Prodigal Son* by Henri Nouwen published and copyright 1992 by Darton, Longman and Todd Ltd and used by permission of the publishers. Extracts from Religious Experience Research Centre archives used by permission of the Religious Experience Research Centre, Westminster College, Oxford OX2 9AT. John Ruysbroeck, *Adornment of Spiritual Marriage*, J.M. Dent (Orion Publishing Group). John R.W. Stott, *The Contemporary Christian*, published by Inter-Varsity Press. Rosemary Sutcliffe, *Blue Remembered Hills*, published by The Bodley Head. John V. Taylor, *The Christlike God*, SCM Press, 1992. 'Love That is Silent' by Jacopone da Todi, translated by Serge and Elizabeth Hughes, used by permission of Paulist Press Inc. C.E. Vulliamy, *John Wesley*, published by Epworth Press and used by permission of the Methodist Publishing House.